accolades for Magical Housekeeping

*"This magical book reminds us that everything is
connected outside and inside: environment and psyche,
style and substance, house and heavens. If you are ready
for positive change, you can't do better than this!"*

—Ana Brett and Ravi Singh, yoga teachers with
several best-selling Kundalini yoga DVDs. Dubbed
"yoga teachers to the stars," their clients have included
Madonna, the Red Hot Chili Peppers, and Sting.

*"Tess Whitehurst shows us that cleaning can be a powerful tool for
personal transformation. Magical Housekeeping incorporates
mantras, angels, faeries, crystals, plant and animal allies. Get
your brooms ready... housekeeping will never be the same again."*

—Ellen Dugan, author of *Cottage Witchery,
Natural Witchery* and *Garden Witch's Herbal*

About the Author

Tess Whitehurst is a lifelong student of the magical arts and an intuitive counselor, energy worker, feng shui consultant, and speaker. Her writings (which have appeared in such places as *New Witch* magazine and Llewellyn's *Magical Almanac*) emphasize perceiving life through a magical lens and advocate self-love, self-expression, and personal freedom. She is also an environmental activist, a (usually) raw vegan, and a kundalini yogini. She lives in Venice, California, with her two cats and musical boyfriend. To learn about her workshops, writings, and appearances, and to sign up for her free monthly newsletter, visit her at www.tesswhitehurst.com.

Simple Charms
& Practical Tips for
Creating a Harmonious Home

MAGICAL
HOUSEKEEPING

Tess Whitehurst

LLEWELLYN PUBLICATIONS
Woodbury, Minnesota

FIRST EDITION
First Printing, 2010

Book design by Rebecca Zins
Cover design by Lisa Novak
Cover images: room © iStockphoto.com/Nicky Gordon,
pentagram © iStockphoto.com/Nicolette Neish
Gesture illustrations by Wen Hsu

Llewellyn Publications is a registered trademark of Llewellyn Worldwide Ltd.

Library of Congress Cataloging-in-Publication Data
Whitehurst, Tess, 1977–
  Magical housekeeping: simple charms & practical tips for creating a
harmonious home / Tess Whitehurst.—1st ed.
      p. cm.
  Includes bibliographical references and index.
  ISBN 978-0-7387-1985-6
  1. Charms. 2. Magic. 3. Parapsychology. 4.
Housekeeping—Miscellanea. I. Title.
  BF1561.W45 2010
  133.4′4—dc22

                                      2010003739

Llewellyn Publications
A Division of Llewellyn Worldwide Ltd.
2143 Wooddale Drive
Woodbury, MN 55125-2989

www.llewellyn.com

Printed in the United States of America

Contents

Acknowledgments

To my mom for teaching me that being myself was the best and only thing that I could possibly be, and for speaking to me in the language of magic since before I was even born.

To my dad for teaching me to question everything, for challenging me to do exactly what I most wanted to do, and for repeatedly saying and demonstrating that "there are more things in heaven and earth, Horatio, than are dreamt of in your philosophy."

To Ted Bruner for every single thing.

To Sedona Ruiz for making those first daring treks with me to Wonderland, Oz, and the Isle of Avalon, and for being my muse and the sister of my soul.

To J. P. Pomposello for giving me the idea that I could write.

To Cheryl Hamada for relaying the divine message that it was time to get to work.

To Mike Milligan and Courtney Lichterman for the generously shared wisdom and countless votes of confidence.

To Jonathan Kirsch for his expert guidance and heart-centered support.

To Denise Linn, Ana Brett, Ravi Singh, Doreen Virtue, Louise Hay, Marina Medici, Karen Kingston, Terah Kathryn Collins, Scott Cunningham, Eckhart Tolle, Byron Katie, Joseph Campbell, Julia Cameron, Allen Ginsberg, Rob Brezsny, and all those whose work helps to dissolve the illusory floodgates to the infinite.

Acknowledgments

To Becky Zins for beautifying this book and profoundly blessing it with her wisdom and expertise.

To Cat Fusca, Elysia Gallo, Amy Martin, Bill Krause, Lisa Novak, Lynne Menturweck, Sally Heuer, and everyone at Llewellyn for so many perfect opportunities, contributions, and gifts.

To the Goddess, Archangel Michael, Archangel Metatron, the fairies, and all the rest of my otherworldly guides and helpers.

And finally, to Smoke, the magic cat who waits for me beyond the veil.

Introduction

Everything is holy! everybody's holy! everywhere is holy!
everyday is in eternity! Everyman's an angel!
—Allen Ginsberg, "Footnote to Howl"

I WAS SITTING under a canopy of oak trees in northern California, listening to a lecture on how to make love charms and herbal aphrodisiacs. Suddenly, seemingly out of nowhere, the teacher stressed the importance of clearing clutter. "Old, stagnant stuff in your home means there is old, stagnant stuff in your mind, body, and emotions. It's *baggage*," she said, "and it complicates your life and relationships."

This was the first time I had thought seriously about the connection between my home and my life. Though I didn't realize it then, learning to recognize this connection was to be an essential key that would powerfully activate my spiritual path and give much-needed direction to my ongoing quest to improve myself and my life. It was in that moment that I started to understand that my state of mind, my relationship with myself, and the way I expressed myself to the world were very closely intertwined with the feelings I had in and about my home. And, because so much of my life was lived in my home, I began to see that it quite literally made up the fabric of my reality.

As I describe in the first chapter, I started by reading *Clear Your Clutter with Feng Shui* by Karen Kingston and consequently began clearing clutter out of my apartment like a madwoman. The lightness and clarity that it brought me was so profound that I almost immediately felt like a different person. For years, I had struggled off and on with depression, discord in my relationship with my boyfriend, family drama, money issues, an "inability" to meditate, acne, a negative body image, confusion about my career path, and general, all-around "bad luck." That all began to dissipate and shift as I continued to clear old, unwanted, and unloved stuff out of my apartment. Most of the negative conditions didn't disappear overnight. In fact, some took quite a while to work through (and a few still reappear at times!), but the stagnant energy wasn't stagnant anymore, and I knew in my heart that the baggage had finally begun to powerfully move out of my life. It was such a relief.

Though I'd been a student of magic and metaphysics for some years before the clutter-clearing rampage, it suddenly all began to make sense on a much deeper level than before. This might sound strange, but the palpable difference I felt as I let go of each bag of clutter was somehow a window into the subtle field that surrounds and fills everything, and connects it all together. I was finally beginning to perceive energy in an experiential way. This made me want to read more about energetic space clearing, and I sought out books that seemed to resonate with what I already felt on a gut level. It was then that I discovered the gentler and more intuitive practices of feng shui, such as those taught by Denise Linn (*Space Clearing A–Z*), Terah Kathryn Collins (*The Western Guide to Feng Shui*), and David Daniel Kennedy (*Feng Shui for Dummies*).

After I had cleared and cleaned like never before, I composed and performed an intense space-clearing and home-blessing ritual that combined the natural magic principles I had been working with for years with the new (to me) space-clearing and feng shui wisdom I'd been studying. And it was definitely intense! I lit candles, invoked the four elements, clapped, burned sage, used chimes, the whole bit. When it was over, I had raised so much energy that the room was spinning. I actually had to lie down for a long breather before I could sufficiently ground myself and return to everyday reality. Though I had performed rituals in the past, actually feeling this amount of power in a tangible way during a ritual was a first for me. And boy, did it create a shift! The room almost seemed to pulsate and sparkle. It was as if someone had increased the wattage in the lights or opened a window that had never been open before.

Now, everywhere I looked in my home, I saw things that I loved and that virtually glowed with positive energy. What had been just an apartment before was now a sacred space that inspired me, nurtured me, and lifted my spirits. And this was just the beginning! In the years following, I attended the Western School of Feng Shui, started my own private feng shui practice, and began writing about and lecturing on the principles that I was now working with on a regular basis. And, best of all, my life was now characterized by a joyful harmony and flow that I had never known before.

As if all this weren't enough, working with the magical energies in my home has led to the continual deepening of my intuition: my ability to sense the energies emanating from objects, the distinctive personalities of plants, and the thoughts and feelings of people and animals. Somewhere along the way

I became a vegan, since I was connecting so deeply with animals and could clearly feel the pain and suffering within animal foods and products. Then I became a raw vegan, since I could sense the healing and consciousness-expanding qualities of live plant foods, and because I felt guided that this would help me to live in blissful harmony with the planet and the universe. Living in this way (at least most of the time, because I do have a few beers or a plate of French fries every now and then) has intensified my intuition and connection with the subtler energetic realms even further, and has no doubt contributed to my insights into the metaphysical qualities of plants, animals, crystals, colors, etc.

My path has also led me to the realization that being environmentally conscious is not just for the sake of the planet. It's for our own sakes: to be grounded in and respectful of all of nature is a prerequisite to true and abiding happiness. And our homes are the perfect places to start—after all, they are our own personal corners of Mother Earth and the only places where we have ultimate jurisdiction over how she is treated. And when we treat her well, she treats us well. Just as we love to give gifts to the people in our lives who appreciate us and are grateful for past gifts we've given them, the earth goddess loves to shower us with her gifts of nurturance and plenty when we respect her and live from a place of gratitude. That's why you'll find that throughout the book, I recommend earth-loving habits such as respecting plants and animals and using soy candles and green cleaning supplies.

Everything is connected, and every inch and component of the physical world is filled with an invisible life force and unique magical energy. I've written this book because I'm certain that every one of us has the inherent ability to sense, change, channel, and direct these energies to create positive conditions and manifest the true desires of our hearts—maybe not overnight, and maybe not in exactly the way we expect, but that would be boring anyway. Besides, living magically is all about the journey, and I've found that it's the most exciting and rewarding journey we could possibly embark upon.

With great love,

Tess

1

Clutter Clearing

EVERYTHING IS CONNECTED. When we look at our homes with this in mind, we see that they are like extensions, or reflections, of our bodies, lives, and emotional landscapes. This is an illustration of Hermes Trismegistus's famous magical precept, "As above, so below." Above, the seen and externally manifested world (our homes), and below, the unseen and internally manifested world (our thoughts, feelings, and experiences), are not only mirrors of each other, but they are also one and the same.

This connection between the seen and the unseen, as it relates to personal dwellings, is something we're already aware of. For example, the next time you watch a movie, notice the homes of the characters. If it's the home of a happy couple, notice the environmental cues that let you know this. You'll probably notice things like warm colors, happy pictures, and fresh flowers. An unhappy couple's home, on the other hand, will probably have cool and muted tones everywhere, hard and shiny surfaces, and austere or sparse decorations. Similarly, a happy character may live in a relatively tidy, pleasingly lit home, while a depressed character's home may be cavelike, cluttered, and lit either too brightly or too dimly. Notice how quickly you make assumptions about the lives of the characters based on their homes. We're able to do this because we're inherently aware that the same patterns are true in real life.

Also, you've possibly already had the experience of clearing out a bunch of old stuff and feeling an amazing increase in your degree of clarity, ease, energy, and joy. These positive feelings come from things like being able to find exactly the item you're looking for, being surrounded exclusively by what you enjoy gazing upon, not having the responsibility of caring for and housing a bunch of stuff you don't especially care for, and opening your closet to see a rack full of clothes that you look great in.

Not only that, but from a magical perspective, clutter represents and holds heavy, stagnant energy that can make it difficult, if not impossible, for you to move forward in life. Releasing clutter breaks up this stagnant energy, allowing your life to flow in a healthier, happier, and more buoyant way.

The first time I did a thorough clutter clearing, I was living in a tiny (but adorable) shoebox apartment in Hollywood with my boyfriend and cat. I'd just read a book called *Clear Your Clutter with Feng Shui* by Karen Kingston, and I'd been transformed into a tornado of simplicity, tearing through drawer after drawer and cupboard after cupboard, throwing out, giving away, repairing what was broken, and finishing unfinished projects. I didn't stop for two weeks, and I threw out or gave away more than eight large trash bags full of clutter. I was amazed that there was even enough room for all the stuff I'd been hoarding. And when I was finished, I started eating healthier (not having clutter in my house made me not want to put clutter in my body), exercising more (the stagnant energy had moved out of my house, and I felt a natural energy and lightness), and feeling more inspired and empowered (I no longer felt like my possessions owned me, and I felt like I had reclaimed my own life and could choose where I wanted to put my attention and energy). I ended up losing ten pounds without trying, and because I had released a bunch of clothes that I didn't feel good in, I created the space for clothes I *did* feel good in. Consequently, I "happened" to receive a huge pile of brand-new hand-me-downs from my cousin, the lead singer of a successful punk rock band, who "happened" to be my exact same size—and who regularly received more free designer clothes than she could possibly wear or fit in her closet.

Clearing clutter is a very powerful practice that helps to align you with the subtle and energetic realms. When you look around your home and tune in with each item, deciding whether it's enhancing your energy or draining your energy, you're powerfully fine-tuning your energy field and the energy field of your home, and "clearing the decks" for magical blessings to swirl into your life.

When clearing clutter, I find it helpful not to worry about what I will use instead. For example, if you don't like your kitchen table and let it go and end up with no kitchen table for a while, sit on the couch or the floor or at the dining room table to eat until you find or magically receive a kitchen table you love. It's safe, and liberating, to dwell in the space in between one kitchen table and another kitchen table, and there's nothing wrong with sitting on the floor for a while to eat your cereal. Of course, don't do anything you're not comfortable with.

If you feel better about keeping the old until you can replace it with the new, go ahead and do that. And sometimes this is more practical, like if you want to replace all your bathroom towels.

Categories of Clutter

The general rule with clutter is, if you don't love it, or don't need it, *get rid of it*—no matter what it is, who gave it to you, how long you've had it, or what it represents. Still, it can be helpful to learn about the different types of clutter so you can perform a clean sweep of your home efficiently and effectively, letting nothing escape your powerfully purifying gaze.

Paper

This category includes old receipts, love notes from past relationships, credit card offers, "to do" lists, warranties for appliances you no longer own, birthday cards from three years ago (or last year), expired coupons or coupons you'll probably never use, etc. Attack any filing cabinets, junk drawers,[*] corners of your bureau, or other places where paper clutter like this tends to accumulate.

Clothes

If it doesn't fit you or you don't absolutely love it, get rid of it. If you're waiting until you lose a few pounds or until you can afford to get new clothes, get rid of it. You deserve to have a closet containing only clothes that look great on you *as you are now*, even if this means having just three outfits in your closet

---

[*] I *do* recommend having a junk drawer, because there are some things that just don't seem to go anywhere else. Just make sure you clear it often.

for a while. Every time you look at clothes you don't like or that you'll wear "someday," your self-esteem suffers, and it consequently becomes harder to lose weight and/or receive abundance. Bravely letting go and making the space for clothes you love is an affirmation of self-love and prosperity consciousness, and when it's done with great faith, you'll have the resources to obtain perfect new clothes exactly when you want or need them.

Books

I like to read all kinds of books, but that doesn't mean I like to *own* all kinds of books. For example, if I were going to live forever, I might consider reading works of fiction more than once—but since there are so many books in the world, and I will never have the time to read them all during this lifetime, I probably will only read most novels and books of short stories only once, though there are some exceptions. For that reason, my library is mostly filled with reference books. For me, this means books about yoga, feng shui, crystals, herbs, trees, magic, etc. For you, it might mean books about fencing, cooking, stargazing, grant writing, or any number of other things. Basically, I keep only the books I will open again, which includes the exceptions to the fiction rule such as *The Mists of Avalon* and *The Complete Works of Shakespeare*. (Again, yours will probably be different.) The rest—the books I read once and will never read again—I check out from the library or purchase and then donate to the library. If you're from a family like mine, the kind that holds on to every book forever no matter what, this might seem like a shocking concept at first, as it did to me. But when you realize how much more space you have, and how much better your house feels when it's not crammed with every book you've ever owned or read, you'll definitely get used to the idea.

Decorations

When a decoration is doing its job, it makes you feel good every time you see it. It brings beauty to the atmosphere and joy to your heart. When it's not doing its job, it's clutter. This includes silk or dried flowers or plants that are past their prime, things you used to love but don't anymore, or things you never loved in the first place. It also includes imagery that makes you feel depressed or portrays a condition you wouldn't like to experience in your own life. For example, no one could honestly deny that *The Scream* by Edvard Munch is an amazing piece of art. However, if you're looking at it every single day, whether you consciously notice it or not, it's affecting your life on a very deep level and is most likely aligning you with feelings of fear, loneliness, danger, and insanity. For this reason, paintings like *The Scream* are best left in the museum. On the other hand, *The Kiss* by Gustav Klimt is not only an amazing piece of art by just about everyone's standards, but, if gazed upon every day, it would most likely infuse your life with feelings of warmth, romance, passion, and joy.

Furniture

If a piece of furniture doesn't fit in your house, and you're holding on to it because it was expensive, it's clutter. If you're sleeping on a bed you shared with a former live-in partner, it's holding the energy of the old relationship and making it difficult for you to manifest a new relationship or a relationship that doesn't remind you of the old one. The same is true for couches and dining room tables. Other furniture that you would want to let go of would be furniture that you don't love, furniture that's uncomfortable to sit on, and furniture that you're always hitting your shin or your toe on.

Gifts

If you don't love something, even if it was a gift, get rid of it! Your house is a very magical and sacred place. Don't bring the energy of guilt into it by holding on to unloved gifts. Respect the gift and the giver by releasing any unloved gifts to someone who will appreciate them.

Food

Get really honest here. Are you ever really going to eat the rest of that mango salsa that's been sitting in the back of your fridge for months? What about the freezer-burned tortillas or that strangely flavored nutrition bar that you accidentally bought? No? Didn't think so.

Car Clutter

This is a big one for me. Things just seem to accumulate in my trunk and back seat. Whenever I do a car clearing, I always feel so much better, and it always seems like my car runs better too (though I'm probably imagining it).

Unfinished Projects or Broken Things

Unfinished projects can make you feel guilty or over-whelmed every time you see them. When you run across them during the clutter-clearing process, either finish them or get rid of them. This would include the sewing project you lost interest in, the scrapbook you never got around to making, or the woodpile you've been meaning to chop into firewood.

The same is true for broken things. Fix them, replace them, or just get rid of them. It makes everything flow better and brings a sense of ease and serenity to every area of your life. This includes squeaky hinges, sticky doors or locks, drawers that fall when you open them, etc. If, however, something is technically broken but it still works and doesn't cause too much hassle (like the lamp that's sitting next to my computer that I turn on and off by twisting the light bulb, or double-sized toaster on my counter that only toasts on one side), don't obsess.

Items with Negative Associations

You might have a perfectly lovely scarf … that was a gift from your psycho ex. Or a gorgeous painting … that was a hand-me-down from the domineering great aunt whom you never got along with. Even if something just reminds you of a time or a person that you'd like to put in the past, consider letting go of it.

How to Know if It's Clutter

Generally, if you don't love, need, or use something, it's time to get rid of it. But if you're not entirely sure if it's clutter or not, here are three simple methods that can help you figure it out:

Method 1: The Mystical Method

Hold it in your hands or place your hands on it. Close your eyes, relax, and take some deep breaths. Sense the subtle energy exchange between you and the object. How do you feel when you tune in to this object? Happy? Sad? Vibrant? Tired? In other words, does it seem to be giving you energy or taking energy from you? Or is it neutral?

If you sense/imagine/feel that it's giving you positive energy, it's not clutter. If you sense/imagine/feel that it's taking positive energy from you, it is clutter. If it's neutral, you might want to move on to method 2 or method 3.

Method 2: The Energetic Bargaining Method

Think about all the energy that you put into housing and caring for this item. First of all, it's taking up expensive real estate in your home—it's occupying space for which you pay good money, and space that might be used for or occupied by something else. Also, consider the upkeep that it requires. For example, you may take time every week to clean it. It might also take a bit of valuable energy from you every time you think about it if it reminds you of a time or person that was not entirely positive (even if you don't think about this consciously) or if it causes you stress or annoyance of any kind. Once you've made a mental tally of your energetic offerings to this item, consider the positive energy it offers to you—is it useful to you, does it make you happy, etc. Then, ask yourself if you feel comfortable with the energetic exchange. Are you getting a good deal? Is it worth it to you to hang on to this item? Or is it clutter?

Method 3: The Imaginary Move Method

Sit near the item, take some deep breaths, and close your eyes. Now, imagine you are moving, and that it's a wonderful feeling! You're so happy to be moving to a new house, and perhaps to a new city, because you know in your heart that you're about to embark on a fresh start that will allow you to redefine yourself and joyfully manifest all the desires of your heart. See yourself hiring movers or renting a moving van and packing up all your beloved items in boxes. Now, open your eyes and look at the item. Do you want to take it with you into this beautiful new life? Does it fit with your most ideal vision for yourself? Is it worth the time and effort of packing it up and moving it? If the answer to any of these questions is no, it's clutter.

After doing an initial, thorough clutter clearing, which could take a day or a month or a year, depending on your past habits, it's important to clear regularly. This is because accumulation has become our way of life. Junk mail, birthday presents, impulse buying, and millions of other clutter channels tend to refresh our collections at a rapid rate. For me, regular clutter clearing means going through all my clothes, books, and papers at least once a month and letting go of all the extras. Every four to six months, I also go through all my cupboards, shelves, the trunk of my car, the refrigerator, etc., to make sure I'm only holding on to things that hold vibrant, helpful energy. I can tell I need to do this when it starts to feel difficult to keep the house clean or when I feel stuck either creatively or emotionally. Once you get in the habit of staying clutter-free, you become more sensitive to energy, which not only enhances your happiness, intuition, and magical workings, but also helps you to notice when a thorough clutter clearing is in order.

Clutter-Clearing Jumpstart Ritual

When you know you're due for a serious clutter clearing, just getting started can sometimes feel like a bit of a drag. But never fear! The clutter-clearing jumpstart ritual is here. All you need is a large white candle (soy or vegetable wax if possible) and a hot cup of a delicious, energizing beverage, such as coffee or black tea (or, if you don't do caffeine, peppermint or ginger tea will work just as well).

Before you prepare the beverage, decide on an area that you're willing to start with. Choose something that doesn't overwhelm you too much but maybe pushes your limits just a tiny bit. I suggest something like a desk or closet, but if this feels like too much, you could even decide that you're willing to start with a single drawer or shelf. Just like in yoga, push yourself a bit, but don't overextend. Only you know your limits.

Once you've decided on this starter area, clap your hands very loudly around the inside or outside of the area to loosen and unstick the energy contained within. Then wash your hands and prepare the beverage. Before lighting the candle, hold it in both hands and focus your attention on it as you say:

> *I triumph over clutter in every way.*
> *I am the master of my domain.*

Light the candle and sit in front of it. Hold the beverage in both hands and focus your attention on it as you say:

> *I now charge this beverage with the energies*
> *of purity, lightness, and motivation.*

Then fully relax as you enjoy the beverage, knowing that you'll be ready and willing (and maybe even excited) to begin your clutter-clearing project as soon as you've finished the last sip. Let the candle continue to burn as you clear, and don't be surprised if you end up clearing out a bit more than you'd planned. Light the candle each time you clear, repeating the ritual if desired.

❧

Clearing Internal Clutter

While clearing clutter out of your physical environment, it's inevitable that your internal clutter (also known as baggage) is going to rise to the surface. This is something we all know on an intuitive level, which, ironically, is often what holds our external clutter in place. Instead of looking at and healing our old, painful issues, we prefer to leave them hidden away in drawers and dark corners of closets, telling ourselves we'll deal with them later.

Below, you'll find descriptions of the three main types of internal clutter, along with suggestions on how to clear each type out of your mind, body, spirit, and/or emotions. You can do this work in tandem with the external clutter clearing, or, if you're having trouble initiating the process, you might like to start on the internal level to begin to loosen and unstick the stagnant energy in your life. No matter which side you approach it from, beginning to dislodge and dissolve the stagnant energy in your life will create a momentum and get everything flowing, like the first ice melting and flowing down from the top of a snowy mountain.

Physical Toxins

Detoxifying your body on a regular basis can help purify you of accumulated toxins that affect not only your body but also your mind and emotions. It's important to get in the habit of detoxifying by drinking at least half your bodyweight in ounces of water every day. I also suggest cutting back on meat and other animal products, white sugar, white flour, and artificial additives, as these hold dense, negative, and unhealthy vibrations and contribute to the accumulation of toxins in the body.

And eat as many fresh fruits and vegetables as possible to nourish your system and help gently move out the toxins. For more on healthy eating habits, check out *Conscious Eating* by Gabriel Cousens and *Eating in the Light* by Doreen Virtue and Becky Prelitz.

Here are some other regular detoxification habits you might like to try:

· ·

Cayenne Cocktail

My friend Jennie Chester Moran, who is a raw food coach, taught me how to make this. (Though I added the agave to the recipe myself.) Not only is it delicious and energizing, it's also extremely detoxifying for your liver and digestive system. I like to drink it immediately upon waking up to get my digestion and metabolism going, but feel free to drink it anytime.

INGREDIENTS:

1 lemon

About ¼ teaspoon cayenne pepper (less
   or more according to your taste)

Stevia (an herbal, calorie-free sweetener) to taste

Agave nectar (a raw, honeylike sweetener) to taste

2 cups water

Use a lemon squeezer to extract the juice from the lemon (only use half if it's a large lemon). In a tall glass, mix all the ingredients.

· ·

Beauty Juice

This drink isn't quite as delicious as the cayenne cocktail, but it's highly nourishing and very purifying for your blood and internal organs. It also has the added benefit of clearing up and beautifying the skin—hence the name.

INGREDIENTS:

> A small handful of each of the following
> dried herbs: burdock root, dandelion
> root, nettles, red clover blossoms
>
> 1 cup aloe vera juice
>
> 5 cups water

Bring a medium-sized pot of water to boil. Add the handful of burdock and the handful of dandelion. Cover, reduce heat, and simmer for 10 minutes. Add the handful of nettles, cover, and simmer for an additional 5 minutes. Remove from heat and add the red clover blossoms. Cover and steep 10 minutes. Strain and cool. Add the aloe vera juice, and drink 8 to 24 ounces per day.

. . . .

Salt Baths

Taking a 40-minute (or longer) bath at least once a week is a great way to release toxins through your pores. Make sure you have plenty of drinking water on hand. Draw a hot bath, and dissolve 2 cups Epsom salts, ¾ cup sea salt, and ½ cup baking soda into the water. Add a few drops of lavender oil for some relaxing and emotionally purifying aromatherapy if desired, and enjoy.

. . . .

Exercise

Regular exercise that works up a sweat—such as running, walking, or dancing—helps get your energy moving and cleanses you from the inside out. Yoga is also very purifying, as it helps stimulate your muscles and internal organs in a way that helps them to release tension and toxins.

Grudges, Grievances, and Old Hurts

We've all, at certain times in the past, been badly hurt and badly treated. For a very long time, I made a point of holding on to my pain and my anger, and on some level I even defined myself by it. But now I can see that whenever I hold on to a hurt or blame someone else for doing something to me, I'm giving away my power. I am, in effect, saying, "I do not have power over my own life. That person (or condition) has power over me, and I am helpless to do anything about it." Beginning to forgive and to let go of these old hurts allows us to take the first step in reclaiming our power and finding peace in our lives. Remember: it's not for other people's sake that we forgive, but for our own.

Not more than a year ago, I experienced the joy of forgiveness in a big way. It started when my long-lost stepfather contacted me online. This man had molested me when I was an adolescent, and when he contacted me I realized that I had been purposely ignoring the strong feelings of victimhood and anger that I was still holding on to after so many years. After a lot of soul searching, I finally found forgiveness and replied to him with a long email, letting him know that his actions were absolutely not okay, but that I realized he must have done them out of a deep shame and self-loathing. I let him know that I had compassion for him and forgave him. (And I actually meant it!) After I sent it, I felt a very deep level of contentment and relief, as if something heavy had been lifted off of my stomach and lungs. Not long after, he responded with a confession and an apology, which was icing on the cake. I felt so empowered that I felt moved to finally let my mom know what had happened, which allowed me to deal with (and eventually release) even more anger—anger that I didn't even realize I had been carrying around. The whole experience unleashed a torrent of forgiveness, and as a result I felt a huge amount of power come rushing back to me. And I had a strong intuitive feeling that bringing the abuse out into the open allowed my mom and former stepfather to heal and release a lot of their old negative energy surrounding the issue as well.

While it can sometimes be immediate, actually doing the work of forgiving and letting go can often take a while, so be patient with yourself. Here's an exercise you can do to get the ball rolling.

. . . .

Keys to Freedom

In your journal or notebook, write "keys to freedom" at the top of the page. Beneath that, make a list of all the people, conditions, and situations that you hold a grudge against. List anything that makes you feel like a victim in any way. Continue writing until you've written down everything you can think of. When you're finished, relax your body and take some deep breaths. Then go through the list, and with each item on the list, close your eyes and bring it into your mind. Once you've conjured up the image or feeling associated with it, mentally tell the person or situation that you're willing to forgive him, her, or it, because you're ready to reclaim the power you've given over to them. You don't have to actually find it in your heart to forgive quite yet, you just have to be *willing* to forgive. (If you find it difficult to even be willing, this is an excellent thing to discover, as a lot of your power must be tied up in this issue. In this case, rise to the challenge and be patient with yourself. You might want to approach the issue from another angle, such as getting counseling or energy healing, or by clearing physical clutter first.) Just being willing to forgive will begin to loosen the negative energy surrounding this issue, which will eventually allow you to get your power back. After the exercise, make a conscious point of fully forgiving the past and moving on with your life. I find it helpful to mentally conjure up as much love and compassion as possible and send it toward any person or situation that I'm having an issue with.

For more support with forgiving and letting go of grudges, grievances, and old hurts, I highly recommend *I Need Your Love—Is That True?* by Byron Katie and Michael Katz. Healing treatments like massage and craniosacral therapy can also really help the forgiveness process.

Limiting Beliefs

Our thoughts and feelings create our reality, and our beliefs underlie our thoughts and feelings, subtly yet powerfully defining them. To use another example from my own life, for many years I worked at jobs I didn't like, and, though I felt like I was constantly working, I was still broke and miserable. Finally (thank Goddess), I started becoming aware of the old beliefs I held that were helping to create and perpetuate this reality for me. While I was growing up, both my parents worked at jobs they weren't too crazy about. In subtle ways, they were also often demonstrating that they were "low on cash" or "worried about money right now." Naturally, through example, I had adopted beliefs like "You have to work at a job you don't like" and "Money is always tight." Once I became aware of these beliefs, I was able to begin to shift and change them. I made a point of noticing people who worked at jobs they loved and who had plenty of money. This helped me to see that my beliefs weren't always true and didn't have to be true for me. I also began repeating affirmations daily, like "I constantly receive abundance from the Infinite Source" and "All doors are open to my perfect career and my perfect success, and I happily walk through them now."

Guilt is another crippling side effect of limiting beliefs, usually beliefs that have the word "should" in them, such as "I should (or shouldn't) have done this or that," "I should be more successful by now," "I should be a better person than I am," etc. Holding on to "should" beliefs allows the toxic energy of guilt to accumulate in our mind and emotions, which creates stagnant and frustrating conditions in our lives. Beginning to love and accept ourselves as we are—and forgiving ourselves for our seeming mistakes and shortcomings—moves us out of that old negative energy and makes room for the new positive energy.

. . . .

A Belief Clearing

My friend Karynne Boese is a life coach, and she taught me this technique. Choose an issue you'd like help with—for example, romance. Then make a list of all the limiting beliefs you hold around that issue. For example, you might write things like:

- Relationships never work.
- I have to give up my freedom and fun to be in a relationship.
- Men suck.

Once you've written down all the limiting beliefs you can think of, take out another page and write an opposing, less limiting belief for each. So, for the ones above, you'd write something like:

- Relationships sometimes work.
- Some relationships might allow me even more freedom and fun than I have now.
- Some men are really great.

Now, for each new belief you've written, write one to three pieces of evidence that they are true. So, staying with the example above, you might write:

- Relationships sometimes work: Aunt Jeana and Uncle Al are really in love, and they've been together for twenty-five years.
- Some relationships might allow me even more freedom and fun than I have now: My partner might challenge me to try new fun things I never would have thought of. Maybe he would watch the dogs sometimes while I went on a yoga retreat.
- Some men are really great: My brother is really great. Grandpa was the sweetest. Martin Luther King, Jr., was one of the most amazing people I can think of.

Now you've already undermined those old limiting beliefs! They might still be there, but they no longer have the stranglehold they once had on your reality. Continue to work with the new beliefs, rereading them every day and continuing to find evidence that they are true.

For more on letting go of limiting beliefs, you might want to check out *You Can Heal Your Life* by Louise Hay and *Loving What Is* by Byron Katie and Stephen Mitchell.

Clearing Clutter Is a Lifelong Pursuit

We're always taking things in: junk mail, gifts, impulse purchases, experiences, new beliefs and ideas, interactions with others, etc. So, once you've cleared to your heart's content and successfully dissolved the stagnant energy in your home, mind, body, and emotions, don't stop there! Make it a habit to purify yourself and your environment on a regular basis. Don't set junk mail down anywhere except the recycling bin. Listen to your words in order to notice any limiting beliefs you might be carrying so that you can release them (e.g., "This always happens to me"). Notice if you're carrying around any old hurts or grudges so that you can forgive. Go through your drawers and closets every month or two to let go of the stuff you don't love or need. Drink lots of water and eat lots of fresh fruit and vegetables. Clutter clearing is a lifelong pursuit and a spiritual practice that continually leads us to greater liberation, lightness, success, abundance, and joy.

Clutter-Clearing Checklist

Physical Clutter		
Paper		
		Old receipts
		Old warranties and other unnecessary documents
		Junk mail
		Old cards and love letters
		Expired coupons
Clothes		
		Clothes that don't fit
		Clothes you don't love
		Clothes that make you feel unattractive or less than stunning
		Clothes you never wear
		Clothes that need to be repaired that you know you'll never repair
Books		
		Any book you'll never open again
Decorations		
		Any decoration that doesn't uplift you or bring you joy
		Any image depicting a condition or feeling you don't want to experience
		Dried or faux flowers or plants that appear faded, dusty, brittle, or overly dead

Furniture	
	Any piece that doesn't fit in your house
	Any bed, couch, or dining table you shared with an ex-partner
	Anything you don't love
	Pieces that injure, trip, or inconvenience you
Gifts	
	Anything you're hanging on to out of guilt or obligation
Food	
	Anything you're honestly never going to eat
Car Clutter	
	Trash
	Anything that doesn't belong in your car
Unfinished Projects	
	Anything you're not going to (honestly) finish within the next month
Broken Things	
	Any broken item you can't or aren't willing to fix (unless it's still useful and convenient and you honestly don't mind that it's a little bit broken)
Items with Negative Associations	
	Gifts or hand-me-downs from people with whom you have negative associations
	Anything that reminds you of a negative situation or period

Internal Clutter	
Physical Toxins	
	Cut back on meat, dairy, eggs, white sugar, white flour, and artificial additives
	Increase intake of water, fresh and dried fruit, fresh vegetables, fruit and vegetable juice, herbal tea, cleansing herbs
	Take sea salt baths
	Exercise
Grudges, Grievances, and Old Hurts	
	Forgive, release, and heal: release old baggage, lighten up, and get your power back!
Limiting Beliefs	
	Our thoughts create our reality and our beliefs define our thoughts: uncover and let go of beliefs that are holding you back from living the life of your dreams.

2

Cleaning

CLEANING HOUSE IS a powerful act of magic. Because (a) everything is connected, and (b) your external environment mirrors your internal environment, when you clean your home, you are also cleaning your mind, body, and spirit. This means that cleaning house allows you to experience increased energy, happiness, clarity, and health, which in turn increases your ability to manifest your desires and bring about ideal conditions in your life.

Not only that, but looking at cleaning in a magical rather than a mundane light transforms every aspect of the experience. It becomes an adventure in vibration-raising—a transcendental, aromatherapeutic, consciousness-expanding practice that activates and empowers the magical energies of your home. And, if you still don't like it, at the very least it should be a little less grueling.

Products

Make sure you've purchased or made earth-friendly cleaning products. Acknowledging and honoring our connection with Mother Earth helps us to feel connected to All That Is. Also, when we honor the earth, the earth honors us. And fairies will be more likely to hang out around our houseplants and gardens when we don't use toxic or harsh chemicals in and around our homes. (More about fairies later.) There are many earth-friendly products on the market and many books about how to make your own. And you can add essential oils and flower essences to your products to lend strength to your intentions. Here are a few ideas:

Essential Oils

As you probably know, essential oils are highly concentrated, all-natural plant aromas that you can find online and in most health food stores. Ten to twenty drops of one or more of these oils in your cleaning products will not only lend a lovely fragrance, they'll also work on an emotional level to positively affect your mood and life experience, as well as the energetic vibration of your home. Many natural cleaning solutions already contain essential oils, so be sure to read the ingredients to get an idea of what magical energies are already at work in the product. Below are a few essential oils that I've found to be especially helpful for cleaning. Be careful while handling them; they're highly concentrated and can sometimes irritate the skin.

Cedar: spirituality, strength, high vibrations

Cinnamon: prosperity, high vibrations (be careful with this one; it can irritate the skin)

Clary Sage: euphoria, clarity

Lavender: relaxation

Lemon: freshness, energy, happiness

Peppermint: energy, love, high vibrations

Rose or Rose Geranium: romance, spirituality, high vibrations

Rosemary: focus, memory

Tangerine: warmth, abundance

Flower Essences

A flower essence might sound like the same thing as an essential oil, but it's actually an entirely different thing. Rather than the scent of a plant, a flower essence is a ready-made potion of sorts. It's the energetic vibration, or unique emotional wisdom of a blossom, preserved in brandy and water. Flower essences are usually used as homeopathic remedies, taken under the tongue or in water, but I also use them in my magical housekeeping practice to change the vibration and feeling in the space. Like essential oils, you can find flower essences online and at most health food stores. Just put two to four drops of a chosen essence in a cleaning solution to bring its therapeutic benefits into your home.

Here are some flower essences that are especially suited for use in cleaning products:

Aspen: helps you feel safe in the space

Bach Rescue Remedy: soothing and clarifying to the energy of a space; removes negativity and turns the tide on challenging energy patterns

Crabapple: creates a cleaner feeling if the area or energy has felt grimy or heavy

Larch: helps you to love your space and take pride in it

Walnut: helps ease the energy during times of change

White Chestnut: creates serenity and calm; good for if you've felt overwhelmed in the space

. . . .

A Broom Blessing

When you're a magical housekeeper, a broom is, of course, not merely a broom—it's a *magical* broom. As it sweeps your floors clean of physical debris, it simultaneously sweeps your home clean of negative energy and energetic debris, which lifts the vibrations and clears the way for positive feelings and conditions. Performing this blessing ritual on your broom (and/or vacuum, which is merely a modernized version of a broom) will fully activate its magical power and consecrate it for your magical purposes.

Please note: it's ideal for the broom or vacuum you bless in this ritual to be brand-new.

INGREDIENTS:

A white sheet or towel

¼ cup salt

One stick frankincense incense

One white or off-white candle

A mister of rose water

On the day or evening of the full moon, assemble the ingredients and lay your broom flat on the white sheet or towel. Light the candle and incense. Lift the broom and bathe it in the smoke of the incense while saying:

I call on the power of air to bless this broom.

Now hold the broom over the flame (being very careful not to set it on fire) and say:

I call on the power of fire to bless this broom.

Lay the broom back onto the cloth and lightly mist it with the rose water (one pump will do) while saying:

I call on the power of water to bless this broom.

Sprinkle the salt over the broom and say:

I call on the power of earth to bless this broom.

When you feel ready, gently shake and dust the salt off the broom and onto the cloth. Lift the broom and hold it in both hands. Close your eyes and feel the awakened magical power of the broom. Next, envision very bright white light flowing down from above, through the top of your head, and throughout your body. See this light also flowing into the broom, as if the broom is an extension of your energy field. After a moment, say:

This broom is now consecrated and
blessed. Blessed be. And so it is.

Extinguish the candle and incense. Shake the salt from the cloth into the bathtub, and put the cloth in the laundry.

Cleaning

While you're cleaning, you might like to play uplifting music to keep the energy moving in a healthy way. You could also burn incense or diffuse essential oils in an oil burner or other scent-diffusing tool to break up and dissolve the old energy that's being released. Also, because your external environment mirrors your internal environment and vice versa, you'll want to drink a lot of water, because cleaning your house will stimulate your body's detoxifying process.

Once you begin to clean, see if you can get into a zone. Listen to the music, smell the essential oils and/or incense, and dissolve into your attentiveness to each and every object and area that you clean. Your attention will bring fresh vibrations and aliveness to each object and area and will align you with the energies of your home. But if your mind wanders, don't worry too much about it.

Some commonsense and magical cleaning tips:

- If it's not dirty, don't clean it. Sounds obvious, but until I learned this, I would sometimes clean things that were already clean out of habit or because I imagined there was an invisible layer of dirt on them. Cleaning only what is dirty saves time, energy, and resources.

- Clean from top to bottom. Clean one room completely and then move on to the next. This also saves time and energy.

- For the environment, use washable instead of disposable whenever possible.

- Periodically, as dirt or dust begins to accrue, clean behind large objects such as dressers, sofas, stoves, and refrigerators, even if you have to have someone help you to move them. This keeps the energy flowing in a healthy way.

- Sweep your doorstep often to keep positive energy flowing into your house.

- Sweep often as a spiritual practice to create clarity and get the energy moving in a healthy way.

- Windows represent the way you see the world, and mirrors represent the way you see yourself. Keep windows and mirrors clean to maintain clear and healthy perspectives.

- The stove represents health and wealth. Keep it clean and sparkling to energize your body and finances.

Magical Floor Washes

Magical floor washes are a powerful way to create the space for what you'd like to experience. They instill a magnetic vibration that helps manifest the desired outcome. Once you've cleaned the floors in the usual ways, you're ready to begin.

. . . .

Prosperity Floor Wash

INGREDIENTS:

> A bucket or similar container
>
> A handful of fresh or one teaspoon dried basil leaves
>
> The peels of one orange
>
> Peppermint essential oil
>
> A mop
>
> A pot or cauldron
>
> A mister (if you have carpet)

Put the basil and orange peel in the pot, fill it with water, and bring to a boil. Cover, reduce the heat, and allow the brew to simmer for 5 minutes. Put water in the bucket and add the brew. Put 7 drops of peppermint oil in the water and stir. Hold your hands over the water, close your eyes, and visualize very bright green light with sparkly gold dust floating around in it coming down from the sky as in a beam of light, entering your head, going into your heart, and moving out through your fingers and the palms of your hands to generously fill the mixture. In your mind's eye, see this light powerfully swirling around in the bucket. If you have carpet, put some of the mixture in the mister. Mop all the hard floors with the mixture. If your doorstep or front porch is made of a mop-friendly material, you might want to mop this area too. Then, lightly mist the carpets with the mixture as well. You can also mist your doorstep with the mixture if you can't mop it.

Home Harmony Floor Wash

INGREDIENTS:

A bucket or similar container

Essential oil of tangerine

Essential oil of grapefruit

Bach Rescue Remedy

1 teaspoon sea salt

A mop

A mister (if you have carpet)

Fill the bucket with water and add 4 drops of tangerine, 4 drops of grapefruit, 4 drops of Rescue Remedy, and 1 teaspoon sea salt. Stir in a clockwise direction. Put your hands in prayer position, close your eyes, and say:

> *Goddess of Hearth and Home, please infuse*
> *this wash with harmonious vibrations and*
> *powerfully establish the qualities of peace, joy,*
> *and happiness within these walls. Thank you!*

Visualize very bright, sparkly, golden-white light filling the mixture. If you have carpet, put some of the mixture in the mister. Mop all the hard floors, including the front porch and doorstep if applicable and possible, and lightly mist the carpets. You can also mist the doorstep/front porch if you were not able to mop that area.

. . . .

Clarity Floor Wash

Use this for cleansing vibrations and clearing the mind.

INGREDIENTS:

A bucket or similar container

White vinegar

Clary sage essential oil

Hornbeam essence

A fluorite crystal

A mop

A mister (if you have carpet)

Cleanse the crystal by running cold water over it for at least thirty seconds or immersing it in dry salt for at least ten minutes. Fill the bucket with water and add ¼ cup white vinegar, 9 drops clary sage oil, 4 drops hornbeam essence, and the cleansed crystal. Stir. Close your eyes and powerfully visualize the liquid completely immersed in very bright white light. If you have carpets, put some of the mixture in the mister. Mop all the hard floors, as well as the front porch and/or doorstep, if possible. Finish by misting the carpets lightly, and, if you weren't able to mop, mist the front porch/doorstep as well.

After Cleaning, Finish with a Personal Cleanse

While cleaning, your body releases toxins through your pores. Also, your aura can sometimes absorb energetic debris. To dissolve and wash away these toxins, take a shower or bath when you're finished cleaning. If you take a bath, put at least ¾ cup of sea salt in it. If you take a shower, use a natural peppermint body wash or soap, or put a few drops of peppermint essential oil into your current body wash. Sea salt and/or peppermint will help dissolve and neutralize all negativity and lift your personal vibrations. Finishing with a personal cleanse is also a great way to express love and appreciation toward yourself for a job well done, and it will leave you with a good feeling, which will help inspire your excitement the next time cleaning day rolls around.

3

Space Clearing

CLUTTER CLEARING AND cleaning help remove both physical and energetic debris from your home and life. Space clearing helps to fine-tune the energy of your home even further by removing any remaining negativity, calling in fresh, abundant, and sparkling energy, and lifting the vibrations to a very high and harmonious level. You'll notice that after performing a space clearing, you'll feel a sense of lightness and buoyancy in your home that you didn't feel before. Inside your walls, arguments, squabbles, confusion, and general negativity will be unlikely to occur, and laughter, inspiration, clarity, joy, and openhearted love will rise to the surface.

There are many ways to clear the space. Whatever method(s) you choose, I suggest opening as many windows and doors as possible before you begin. This is because what you'll be doing is creating healthy movement in the energy flow. When the energy has more places to flow, it can flow faster and fresh energy can flow in more easily and abundantly.

Below, I'll introduce some simple components of space clearing, which you can do alone or in concert with each other.

Then I'll describe a more complete space-clearing ritual that incorporates a number of the components in order to thoroughly clear the energy and raise the vibrations.

Noisemaking

Clapping

Clapping loudly in the corners and around the perimeter of rooms loosens and breaks apart stuck energy. When you're finished clapping, make sure to wash your hands to cleanse them of any negativity they may have absorbed.

Rattles, Drums, and Tambourines

These work much like clapping by unsticking negativity and heaviness and getting the energy flowing in a healthy way. Move throughout the space with the noisemaker, concentrating on corners, dark spots, and the perimeters of rooms.

Chimes and Bells

Chimes and bells raise the vibrations and fill rooms with sweetness and light. Choose chimes and bells with sounds you really love. Ring or chime them at least once in each room and/or area.

Chanting

Slowly and fully chanting the sound "Om" at least three times in each room and area can gently clear negativity and powerfully lift the vibrations in each room. Make sure you breathe deeply, focus, and hold your hands at your heart in prayer position as you do so, paying attention to each part of the chant—the silence as well as each part of the sound: "ah," "oh," and "mmm."

Smudging

White Sage

A bundle of white sage, also known as a sage wand or smudge stick, can powerfully lift and clear the energy of a space when burned like incense around the room. As you light it, acknowledge the spirit of sage, and thank it for offering its leaves for your use. Be very aware of fire safety, holding a dish under the bundle while it burns. Move around each room and area in a counterclockwise direction in the Northern Hemisphere and a clockwise direction in the Southern. Finish by moving the smudge stick around your body to cleanse your aura.

Desert Sage or Sage Brush

This is burned exactly like white sage, but its energy is different: while white sage is a powerful cleanser and spiritual vibration-raiser, desert sage has a more playful energy. It's used as a "road opener" and can powerfully open new and unexpected doors in your life when you feel stuck in any way. It's aligned with the energy of Coyote, the divine trickster of Native American mythology. Because of its trickster energy, it can help you find a way or manifest a door out of thin air. Additionally, it has a very comforting scent and can help ground you and make you feel safe and protected. Use it like white sage but know that it will infuse your home with more playful vibrations and may cause unexpected (but positive) pathways to open in your life. Remember to finish by smudging your body to let your aura reap the benefits of the herb as well.

Sweetgrass

In the form of a braid of long, dried grass, sweetgrass is burned like incense. You can also sometimes find it in incense form. Like sage, call on its spirit as you light it, and thank it for offering itself for your use. Sweetgrass raises vibrations by calling in sweet spirits of deceased loved ones, angels, fairies, and other helpful beings. You don't need to move around in each room; just stand near the center of each room and mentally summon sweet and helpful spirits to enter.

Other Smudgeables

You can also smudge with a number of other incenses. Cedar and frankincense work in a similar way to white sage by lifting, clearing, and infusing the space with highly spiritual vibrations. Copal simultaneously clears and calls in sweet spirits. Nag Champa gently calls in good energy by creating the type of vibration that attracts sweet spirits and setting a spiritual tone. Simply burning these incenses in a single location during a cleansing is also effective. We'll talk more about smudging in chapter 10.

Mists

Misting an area with rose water fills it with love, sweetness, and high vibrations. You can also create or buy a natural mist made with one or more essential oils to clear and uplift. Lemon, orange, tangerine, rosemary, peppermint, cedar, eucalyptus, and lavender would all be good choices. In chapter 10, you'll find a more complete compendium of magical and aromatherapeutic oils and mists.

Visualizations

Vacuum Space-Clearing Visualization

If you only have a minute, or if you have company over and you want to conceal your space-clearing activities, you might like to try this quick (yet powerful) mental space clearing. Sit with your spine straight and relax. Close your eyes and take some deep breaths. When you're ready, visualize a sphere of very bright white light filling and completely encompassing your house. See/sense/imagine this light penetrating the walls and objects and transforming everything into light. Now, visualize a huge vacuum made of light moving through this sphere and fine-tuning/brightening the light by vacuuming up any darkness, stuckness, or negative energy of any kind. I like to visualize something like a cosmic vacuum attachment tube coming down from the heavens, but you can make your vacuum appear however you want, as long as it's powerful for you.

Elemental Space-Clearing Visualization

If you'd prefer to incorporate the elements earth, air, fire, and water in your space-clearing visualization, this would be a good one to do. Relax and get in touch with the earth element. You might like to think about the smell of fresh, clean soil after it rains or the feeling of the cool earth under your bare feet. Once you feel connected to the earth element, visualize the earth under your home. Visualize any negativity in your home moving downward and being absorbed into the earth below, where it's composted and purified. Next, get in touch with the air element. You might envision wind blowing through trees or imagine that you're a bird flying high in the sky. When you feel connected with the air element, visualize / feel a clean, fresh breeze blowing through your entire home, loosening and carrying off stuck and heavy energy while filling it with bright, sparkly light like the light of the sunrise. Now get in touch with the fire element. You might envision a wildfire sweeping across a plain or a raging bonfire at a campsite. When you feel ready, envision fiery energy and light moving through your home, burning away and purifying all negativity. Finally, get in touch with the energy of water. You might call up the sound, scent, and appearance of ocean waves or imagine yourself swimming in the depths of the sea. Once you feel aligned with water, send cool waves of salty ocean water through your entire home and know that they're gently and powerfully washing away all negativity. When you're finished, thank each element individually, take a few more moments to relax, and open your eyes.

A Thorough Space Clearing

The more you practice magical housekeeping, the more in tune you'll be with the energy of your home. In the same way that you know when it's time to take a shower, you'll know when your home needs a little space clearing. But in general, a thorough space clearing like the one below would be good to do at least once a month. Quickie clearings (something informal, like a quick clap or smudge) can be done once a week. And, if you're like me, you might like to do a space-clearing visualization every day as a part of your daily meditation.

INGREDIENTS:

A white soy or vegetable wax or tealight candle for
every room and area (like halls and stairways)

A small plate or platelike candleholder for every room

Sea salt

A bundle of white sage (see above)

Rose water in a mister

Optional: a bell or chime

Assemble all the ingredients in a central location. If you like, you can say a prayer over the ingredients, asking that they be charged with your intention to clear the energy in your space. You can then, if you like, visualize them being filled with very bright white light.

In the room you're in, place one candle on a plate or candle-holder in a central location. Create a ring of sea salt around the candle on the plate, and light the candle. Repeat this process in every room and area. The fire from the candle will burn away negativity and stuck energy, while the salt will absorb any excess.

Go back to the first room and begin clapping loudly around the perimeter of the space, paying special attention to the corners, dark spots, and anywhere else you might imagine that energy could get stuck or stagnant. Repeat in every room and area. This will loosen stuck energy and allow it to be cleared away.

In the first room, open as many windows as possible (if you only just barely crack one, that's okay too). Then light the sage bundle and shake until the flame goes out so that it's smoking. Walk around the perimeter of the room, moving the smoke around to dissolve negativity and lift vibrations. Repeat in every room and area, and extinguish the sage with water or by sealing it in a jar or under an upside-down glass.

Now, go back to the first room and close the windows. Go around the perimeter of the space misting with the rose water to raise the vibrations, add sweetness, and further clear the energy. Repeat in every room and area.

Optional: ring the chime or bell in each room/area to clear, attune, and infuse each room with a high vibratory tone.

Allow the tealights to burn all the way down, or, if you need to be somewhere, let them burn for as long as you can and then extinguish them. You can use the leftover candles for your oil burner, or, if there's enough of them left, you can use them again the next time you perform a thorough space clearing.

Flush the salt down the toilet or pour it down the sink. Wash the plates thoroughly before you use them for something else.

Finish with a shower or bath to cleanse your personal energy, and then eat something with complex carbohydrates like an apple, banana, rice, cereal, nuts, or beans. The shower will clear your aura of any negativity you may have absorbed, and the food will ground you after your magical working.

4

Harmonious Positions

IN EVERY HOME, there are key places: cornerstones of power and opportunities to intensify and preserve the potency of the magic that flows within and around the walls. This chapter is about becoming aware of these places and positioning yourself and your home accordingly.

Your Home's Magical Floor Plan

Our homes, like our bodies, have auras, or energy fields. Within these energy fields, there are specific areas, or what we'll call "power centers," that correspond with specific areas of our lives. This is a lot like the chakra system of the body. The placement of the power centers is derived from the teachings of feng shui, and feng shui derives it from an ancient and universal magical and mathematical tool called the magic square. In the I Ching (said to be the oldest of all books), the magic square is called the *lo shu*, and in ceremonial magic it's called the square of Saturn.

Map of the Power Centers

Gratitude & Prosperity	Radiance & Reputation	Love & Marriage
Health & Family Relationships	Synergy, Balance & Bliss	Creativity & Playfulness
Serenity & Self-Love	Career & Life Path	Synchronicity & Miracles

↑ Main Entrance ↑

Floor Plan Analysis

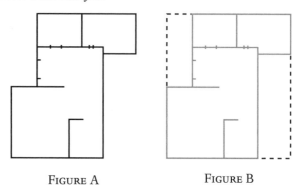

Figure A   Figure B

As magical housekeepers, it's helpful for us to know where these power centers are so that, whenever possible, we can choose room usage and décor accordingly. For example, if you find you have a room in the love and marriage area that could be either a home office or a bedroom, you'd be better off making it a bedroom. You can also use your knowledge of the power centers to make design choices that empower your magical intentions. For example, you might like to place a luxurious green throw blanket in the gratitude and prosperity area to increase your wealth, or romantic imagery in the love and marriage area to enhance your love life. And, once you know the power centers of your home, to intensify the power of your magic you can place magical objects like charms, crystals, or altars (as will be described in later chapters) in the areas that correspond most closely with their purposes.

Ready to discover your home's power centers? Here we go!

- Obtain or create a simple, close-to-scale floor plan drawing of your home or apartment. This does not need to include window or furniture placement and should include any of the following attached features: balconies, covered or raised patios, decks or porches, and garages (see Figure A, left).

- (Skip this step if the outline of your floor plan is a perfect rectangle or square.) Using a ruler and pencil, extend the farthest edges of each side of the main floor of your home so that your entire floor plan is contained within a perfect rectangle or square (see Figure B, left).

- Now, using the ruler, divide each side of the square or rectangle into even thirds. Using these measurements as a guide, now draw a tic-tac-toe board over the floor plan, dividing it into nine equal squares.

- Locate the front door (as intended by the architect—not simply the door you use most often), and draw a small arrow to indicate the direction that people are moving when they enter through it. Rotate the page if necessary so that the arrow at the front door is pointing up (see below).

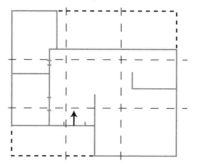

- Look at the diagram on the next page and write the appropriate power center titles on each square. (*Please note:* for additional floors, each power center continues directly above or below the power centers on the main floor.)

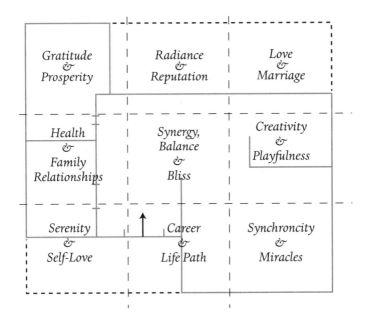

Key to the Power Centers

Gratitude & Prosperity: wealth, luxury, and the feeling that you're perfectly safe and perfectly provided for

Radiance & Reputation: how you are seen and known in the world

Love & Marriage: romance

Health & Family Relationships: physical health, cycles of life, family, elders, ancestors

Synergy, Balance & Bliss: the hub of the wheel of life and the mingling and mixing of all energies

Creativity & Playfulness: joy, whimsy, fertility, babies and children, new projects, prolific creativity

Serenity & Self-Love: stillness, meditation, exercise, rest, joyful study

Career & Life Path: being deeply in alignment with one's inner truth and life purpose

Synchronicity & Miracles: helpful connections, safe travel, divine assistance

The Front Door

Doors are very magical things, especially doors that take you from one realm to another realm. And your front door does just that, not only because it separates the outside from the inside, but also because, as a magical housekeeper, your home exists on an elevated plane of existence and is a magical realm unto itself. For this reason, your front door should be (as author Terah Kathryn Collins says) entrance-ing. It is a magical tool for drawing blessings of every variety into your home. It also dictates the quality, quantity, and vibration of energy that enters.

(*Note:* if you live in an apartment and have very little freedom to change the outside appearance of your door, don't worry! Just do what you can. There are plenty of other ways to call magical energy into your home.)

Clear the Way

Energy flows like water from the outside of your home to the inside via your front door. With this in mind, is anything blocking the flow? Just to give you an idea of what I'm talking about, any of the following things would obstruct the free flow of blessings into your home and life:

- A large potted tree partially blocking the view of the door from the street

- A stone angel statue that you have to make sure to step around so you don't hit your shins or stub your toe

- A table just inside the house, making it impossible to open the front door all the way

Ideally, your front door, and the pathway to your front door, should not be blocked or crowded in any way. Additionally, the door should be free to express its full range of motion. This clears the way for a healthy portion of positive energy (and this means blessings, abundance, happiness, etc.) to enter your home.

Make It Sparkle

It's great if your front door itself is beautiful and in some way enchanting and inspiring. You might, for example, feel like painting it a vibrant and magically selected color. If you do, here are some color ideas:

Royal Blue: Said to be "the" door color for magical folk. Brings a deep, watery, whimsical, and otherworldly vibration to the home.

Red: The classic feng shui door color; very protective and energizing. Calls in blessings and celebrations.

Green or Teal: These door colors summon wealth and prosperity to your doorstep. They also enhance health.

Black: This door color feels powerful and strong. Black lends strength and authority to the residents and brings deeper alignment with one's ideal career.

If a colorful door isn't your thing, you might like to have a door that otherwise speaks to your personal sense of beauty and charm, like something with an appealing wood finish, carved design, or stained glass window, for example. Or, if you have simple and classic tastes, a white or off-white door will do nicely—just make sure it's as attractive as possible. If you're the funky-artsy type (like I am—how'd you guess?), you might enjoy adding mirrored tiles or jewels. Basically, if your front door isn't utterly enchanting, see if you can find a way to enhance it that fits your budget and style. And keep in mind that the appearance and feel of your front door will dictate the quality of energy and blessings that you draw into your life.

Of course, if the hinges squeak, oil them. If the door sticks or you have to jiggle the key, fix it. If the windows are dirty, wash them. After all, your front door is one of your most powerful tools as a magical housekeeper. Just as you wouldn't want a broken or crooked magic wand, you also wouldn't want a less than perfectly functioning or less than sparkling front door.

Get a doormat that you love too! It's best if it feels uplifting and welcoming, so that it lifts spirits and calls in the most positive energy possible. And do yourself a favor: don't get one of those thick shedding ones that get soggy and cause coarse hairs to get tracked all over the house! (When will those go out of style, anyway? And how did they ever get to be *in* style?) It's best to choose something both beautiful and functional. For example, I love those mats made out of actual river rocks. Talk about magical! They're like an invitation for clean, clear energy to come rushing harmoniously into your home like a sparkling river.

Add Some Life

As long as it's not restricting the free flow of energy (and people) into the house, a small or medium-sized potted plant or two, or a Goddess, Buddha, fairy, or animal statue can enliven and set the tone for the energy entering the house. Plants and statues can also act as greeters and guardians for the household.

Wind chimes, if you like them, purify and uplift vibrations, and create a positive energetic shift from one realm (outside) to the next (inside). If you choose to hang a wind chime near your front door, you might like to bless your wind chime by performing a ritual like the one below.

. . . .

Wind Chime Empowerment Ritual

This powerful ritual will enchant your wind chime so that it will create an atmosphere of magic and miracles in your home while calling in beautiful blessings every time it chimes. I must warn you that whether you're a morning person or a night owl, you might find this ritual to be a bit of a challenge, because when you perform it, you have to stay up late and get up early. But believe me, it's worth it!

Choose a metal wind chime that makes a sound you love. On the day *before* the exact day of the full moon, between 11 AM and 2 PM, lay the chime on a clean white cloth and place it outside in full sunlight. Allow it to bask in the light for about 15–20 minutes. This will purify it and empower it with the strong and beneficial energy of the sun. Then wrap it in the cloth and set it inside until night. When the moon comes out, take the chime out again and lay it on the cloth in full moonlight. Allow it to bask in the moonlight for about 30–45 minutes. This will imbue it with the cool and receptive energy of the moon. Once more, wrap it in the cloth and bring it inside. Wake up just before sunrise the next day (this will be the day of the full moon). Take the chime outside and prepare to hang it somewhere near your front door. Face the rising sun if possible. Just as the sun peeks up over the horizon, hang the chime. Then gaze at the chime as you say:

> *Sun and moon together chime*
> *Door of night to morning time*
> *Endless blessings shall abound*
> *As you share your magic sound.*

Open It Up

If you rarely open your actual front door, you're restricting the amount of energy and blessings that can enter your home. If it's not convenient for you to use your front door, just make a habit of opening the door daily or almost daily, perhaps to get the mail or water the yard.

The Power Position

As much as possible, sit so that you can see the main door(s) to the room you're in. It's also good if you're seated a reasonable distance away from the door. This helps you feel safer, clearer, and more powerful. This is especially important for places where you spend a lot of time, such as desks and couches. If this isn't possible, position a mirror so that you can see behind you while you sit. For dining areas and other multi-person seating situations, when at least one adult in the group is easily able to see the door, everyone else will feel safe because they'll be confident that someone is looking out behind them. Notice this the next time you're seated in a restaurant with your back to the door. On a subtle level, you're putting your trust in your companion(s) to "watch your back."

When you discover the power positions in your home and make a habit of sitting in them, you'll feel that you have more power and confidence in every area of your life.

The Bedroom

The more research is done on sleep, the more we discover just how important it is. A good night's sleep is absolutely imperative for our moods, motor skills, reaction time, and thought processes. Not only that, but dreamtime is a bridge to our higher selves, messages from the Divine, creative problem solving, and healing on many levels. So, in the magical home, the bedroom is a place to refresh, revitalize, and restore, as well as rest our bodies while our minds and spirits receive healing and messages from other realms. As if that weren't enough, the bedroom also has everything to do with romance. When our bedrooms are filled with passion, receptivity, and love, so are our hearts and our relationships. (Even if you're not interested in a relationship, romance and receptivity are necessary ingredients for inspiration and joy.) And so sleep and romance, two of the most important of all considerations, must be simultaneously honored when it comes to magical housekeeping in the bedroom.

First, let's talk about the bed. Obviously, it should be very comfortable. A bed with a substantial headboard is best because it helps us to feel safe and protected. Wood is the best material for the headboard because of the simultaneously light and grounded way it conducts energy.

Ideally, the entire bed, but at the very least the mattress and box spring, should be purchased brand-new. Then the mattress should be replaced at least every four years and after divorces, breakups, and serious or long-term physical or mental illnesses. This is because beds powerfully absorb and hold energy, and it's important not to sleep on old, worn-out energy patterns, whether they're our own or someone else's. We'll not only sleep better this way, we'll also avoid living out some sort of condition or situation that isn't us anymore—or never was us in the first place. If it's not possible to replace your bed or mattress right away, and you feel you might be sleeping on some old, negative patterns, then you definitely want to perform the following bed-cleansing ritual ASAP.

. . . .

Bed-Cleansing Ritual

INGREDIENTS:

> 4 white or off-white soy tealight candles in jars
>
> 40 white roses (or at least a dozen)
>
> A mister of rose water

In the evening, when the moon is between full and new, move the bed away from the wall and remove all the bedding. (You might want to take this time to throw the bedding in the laundry, as you'll want it to be freshly cleaned before you replace it.) Place a candle on the ground at each corner. Be very aware of fire safety. Light each candle and turn out the electric lights. Pull out all the rose petals and spread them on top of the bare mattress. Stand over the bed, put your hands in prayer position, close your eyes, and ask for forty angels to powerfully cleanse the energy of your bed and remove all negativity. Visualize the light from the candles expanding until the entire bed is transformed into sparkling golden-white light. Know that this light is burning away and transmuting all old and stagnant energy and replacing it with fresh, new, vibrant energy. Allow the candles to safely burn for at least forty minutes. Then remove the candles and petals, and mist the mattress and box spring lightly with rose water. Bury the petals or scatter them at the base of a tree. Dispose of the candles.

A Few Additional Bed Concerns

Bedding is very important; 100% natural fiber sheets are the healthiest for you and the planet, and are also the most comfortable. Also, for quality sleep, a solid color is best for sheets; for romance, choose a warm or earthy color—this would include any shade of red, orange, pink, yellow, brown, beige, or a darker shade of cream. For some people, brighter colors such as red or bright pink or orange might be overly stimulating, so go for a more muted tone if you tend to have trouble sleeping due to overexcitement or anxiety. (Check the appendix for specific magical properties of colors.) Also choose a warm or earthy color for the rest of the bedding. It's okay to bring in other colors, such as blue, green, or black—just make sure they're present in the form of light accents, such as a couple of small throw pillows or a throw blanket. This is because these colors are cooling and are not conducive to coziness in the bed or warmth in the relationship.

There's not always a "perfect" place in any given bedroom for the bed. But see if you can find the place in the room that fits the highest possible number of the following criteria. If you have to decide between one or another, consider the reasons for the suggestions and go with your gut.

- Place the head against a solid wall. This is because windows or doors behind you while you sleep can make you feel unsafe. If you must put the bed against a window or windows, or against a wall with windows, hang substantial curtains and close them at night.

- Place the bed so that you can see the door but it's not too close to you. This is the power position (see page 54).

- Place the bed so that your feet are not pointing directly at a door. This position can feel a bit unstable, like there's a trap door beneath your feet as you stand. A door elsewhere in the wall opposite your feet is fine, just try not to sleep so that your feet are like an arrow pointing at a door. If you must, make sure the door is closed.

- Place the bed so that you can get in and out of both sides. This way, the energy flows around it in a healthy manner, and it also allows for equality in a shared bed situation and creates the space for a partner if you're not already in a relationship. For these same reasons, I also recommend having two nightstands and two lamps, one on each side of the bed, either matching or comparable in size and stature.

One last word on the bed: don't store anything under it. It's important for energy to flow in a healthy way around and under you while you're in bed. When stuff is under the bed, it feels stagnant. If you've cleared all your clutter (see chapter 1) and you still feel that you absolutely must use the area under the bed for storage space, use it for linens—and then, if you begin to notice that you never seem to use those linens, get rid of them. The longer they sit without being touched, the more stagnant the energy under your bed will become.

More Important Bedroom Tips

- Only display photos of your current relationship (if you have one). Pictures of other people are like those people staring at you while you're in bed; needless to say, this is not conducive to intimacy.

- Hang pictures that are relaxing and romantic.

- Go light on the decorations, books, and doo-dads. Too many little things can be distracting and unsettling while you're trying to sleep.

- Lose the exercise equipment. It's not relaxing or romantic, and chances are you never use it anyway. And if you do, you probably fantasize about going back to bed the whole time. If it absolutely must be in this room, cover it attractively while it's not in use.

- Make sure that the lighting is pleasing.

- Jesus, Buddha, and the Virgin Mary are great, but please leave them out of the bedroom. This goes for other figures and symbols associated with chastity and/or solitude as well, such as a Christian cross or a lone wolf.

- If you can put your desk somewhere else, do it. It's best to limit your bedroom activity to rest and intimacy.

- If you have trouble sleeping or would like to improve your dreams, try creating a sleep charm like the one below.

. . . .

Sweet Dreams Charm for a Good Night's Sleep

Important note: before you create this charm, take a look at your bedroom and make sure you've created the space for a good night's rest. Clear any excess clutter and move things that remind you of work or other daytime activities. Also, mirrors are highly energizing and can be somewhat unsettling in the dark, so try covering your mirrors at night with sheets or table cloths, and if this seems to help, try curtaining them, finding attractive scarves to cover them with at night, or removing them altogether.

INGREDIENTS:

1 small amethyst cluster (tumbled amethyst or an amethyst point will work too)

A rectangle of white or off-white flannel (for size considerations, see below)

Dried valerian root

Dried chamomile

Essential oil of chamomile

A needle and thread

A white or off-white candle (ideally soy or vegetable wax) with holder

Cleanse the amethyst by running it under cold water or burning white sage smoke around it. (See chapter 6 for more on cleansing crystals.) Assemble all the ingredients. Light the candle. Hold your hands over the ingredients and charge them with your intention by visualizing them being filled with sparkly purple light. Know that this is the light of deep and restful sleep, and see/feel/visualize the ingredients pulsating and swirling with this energy. Now, sew a tiny little pillow for the amethyst. Make it big enough so that the amethyst will be able to rest comfortably on it, like a cat on a cat bed. Stuff the pillow lightly with the chamomile and valerian, and sew it closed. Then place the amethyst on top of the pillow. Hold the pillow with the amethyst in both hands and say:

> *Purple light of restful sleep*
> *Happy dreams and comfort deep*
> *Fill this bedroom all the night*
> *As I (we) dream till morning light.*

Feel the magic working, and imagine the wonderful feeling of waking up rested from a good night's sleep. Extinguish the candle and place the charm near your bed, ideally on a nightstand.

The Stove

The stove is a very powerful location. It's the place where the abundance of the earth in the form of food is warmed and prepared for our nourishment. In this way, it's symbolic of the wealth of the household (this is true even if you're like me and prefer your food raw, although for raw foodists a dehydrator and/or Vitamix blender might be regarded as similarly magical). For this reason, it's very important that the stove is clean, that all the burners work, and that it's generally in good repair. It's also a good idea to rotate the burner usage so that all burners get used. This activates the fullness of the power of your stove.

Whether or not you use your stove for food preparation, preparing food at home is a very magical act. It connects you with the bounty of the earth and inspires you with gratitude as it grounds your energy, gets you into your body and out of your head, and relaxes your mind. You can also say prayers and direct positive energy toward the food, which you then internalize as you eat it. But, because the stove is such a powerful place in the home, if you don't use the stove to cook, consider getting a teakettle and using the burners on a regular basis to make tea.

Also, if possible, hang a mirror on the wall over your stove. This energizes the area, helps you to feel safer while you cook (which infuses the food with more positive vibes), and symbolically doubles the positive energy of the stove. And it's easier to keep clean than you might think.

If you like, you can enhance and activate the energy of the stove by placing a lit candle or bowl of oranges on it when it's not in use. By employing a simple prayer or invocation, you can empower the candle or fruit bowl with a specific intention, such as increasing abundance or household happiness. You can also draw upon the power of your stove to create good luck and abundance (and delicious cookies) by performing the following ritual.

. . . .

Oatmeal Cookie Ritual for Abundance and Luck

The recipe used in this spell is my favorite cookie recipe, and it's adapted from *The Garden of Vegan* by Tanya Barnard and Sarah Kramer. Everyone loves these cookies, vegan or no.

INGREDIENTS:

   ¾ cup spelt or whole wheat flour

   ½ cup organic sugar

   2 cups rolled oats

   ½ teaspoon baking soda

   ½ teaspoon baking powder

   ¼ teaspoon cinnamon

   ½ teaspoon salt

   ⅓ cup soft tofu

   ⅓ cup canola oil

   ½ cup agave nectar or maple syrup

   1 tablespoon vanilla extract

   1 cup chocolate chips

Preheat the oven to 350 degrees. After you turn the knob to preheat, place your open palms on the top of the stove and say:

> *I now summon and activate the lucky, prosperous, and life-sustaining energies that live within this stove.*

In a large bowl, stir together the flour, sugar, oats, baking soda, baking powder, cinnamon, and salt. In a blender or food processor, blend the tofu, oil, agave or syrup, and vanilla. Pour the tofu mixture into the flour mixture and stir in a clockwise direction. As you stir, mentally or out loud repeat the words "health, wealth, joy, abundance, luck" over and over until blended.

Add the chocolate chips and continue to stir while repeating mentally or aloud, "Life is sweet, and all is well." Once the chocolate chips are well incorporated, spoon heaping spoonfuls of dough onto a greased cookie sheet and place it in the oven. Just before you close the door, blow three kisses into the oven.

Bake for 12–15 minutes or until the edges are browned. Eat and share with whomever you'd like to bless with abundance and luck. If you have the pleasure of partaking in the cookies with someone else, it might be fun not to mention anything about their magical nature and observe the effect they have on the eater(s), some of which will almost definitely be immediate.

The Fireplace

The fireplace was the original TV. It was the focal point and gathering place of the household. Like the heart of a home, its light and warmth brought homes to life (the word "hearth" is only one additional letter). If you're lucky enough to have a fireplace, I suggest reclaiming its ancient prominence. Make sure that it's in good repair, and light it often during the fall and winter months. When it's warmer out, you can place candles or plants in and around it to keep its energy alive.

To balance the fire energy, activate the area, and contain positive energy within the space, hang a mirror over the fireplace if possible. Also make sure you don't decorate the area immediately surrounding the fireplace with dried flowers or too many flammable-looking things, as it can appear parched and create feelings of exhaustion and thirst.

The fireplace is an excellent place to perform banishing, releasing, and purification rituals. If you have an old habit, limiting belief, discordant situation, or recurring challenge that you're fed up with and you'd like to banish once and for all, you might try the following ritual.

Fireplace Banishing Ritual

Sometime when you have the house to yourself, anytime between the full moon and the new moon, at midnight if possible, start a fire in the fireplace. On a piece of paper, write or draw something that represents the issue, belief, or situation you'd like to banish. Really make it meaningful to you. For example, when I was younger, I was held at gunpoint. For some time after this, I felt afraid to even leave my house by myself. After over a year of living with this debilitating fear, I decided it was time to banish the power this memory had over me. So, before performing this fireplace ritual, I drew a picture of the man who had held me at gunpoint, gun and all. I tried to make it as scary as I could so that it would really represent the power that this man still seemed to wield in my mind. You could also write a poem or journal entry, find an actual photo of yourself that represents the condition or issue, or just write a word or two, like "guilt," "food addiction," or "money fears."

Once you've done this, stand in front of the fire while holding your paper representation in both hands. Take a moment and tune in with the issue. Feel the issue in your hands, and feel it becoming very heavy and cumbersome. Sense what a drag it is to have it in your energy field. Bring up the emotions associated with the issue and really get tired of carrying them around with you all the time. Once you've done this, shift your attention to the flames. Sense how purifying they are and how bright. Contemplate their ability to immediately transform old, dull, lifeless matter into powerful energy and light. Then throw your representation into the flames and watch it burn. Know that its negativity is now being powerfully transmuted for your highest benefit. Feel light and free, and know that you no longer carry the weight of the issue or condition. Express gratitude to the flames. Next, if you feel like it, I highly recommend putting on some empowering music and dancing near the fire to celebrate your new lightness and joy. (You might consider "We Will Rock You" by Queen, "I Will Survive" by Gloria Gaynor, and "What I Got" by Sublime—but of course any song or genre that resonates for you will work. Alternatively, employing a drum-playing friend would be awesome too.) Also, because you've released so much negativity, you'll want to make sure to drink at least one large glass of water after the ritual to help further purify toxins from your body and energy field.

Television Sets

To me, an excessively huge television always seems to ruin the magical vibe. If one or more family members absolutely insist on a man-eating screen, see if you can relegate it to a game room or den, so that you don't have to give up your living room to the talking heads, drama mamas, and corporate sponsors.

Also, I highly recommend covering all TVs when they're not in use. This could be with a piece of furniture made expressly for this purpose, or a simple scarf or cloth. Even when a TV is off, it brings a very non-magical feeling into the room. It's like a dead spot and can create subtle feelings of loneliness and incompleteness until it's turned on. As you might imagine, this greatly encourages excessive TV watching. As an alternative, I sometimes like to leave my TV uncovered but pop in a DVD of a fireplace or an underwater seascape. This creates an interesting and serene focal point that feels alive but not overpowering.

5

The Three Secrets Empowerment

IN ESSENCE, THE three secrets empowerment is the stereo-typical image of a magician practicing magic. With great authority and power, the magician moves a wand or a hand or an eye in a certain way. This is secret number one: gesture. As she does this, she says a magic word or words—a.k.a. secret number two: vocalization. But of course, she must simultane-ously concentrate on and fully expect her intended outcome, which brings us to secret number three: visualization/expecta-tion. We'll go into these more fully in just a moment, but just to review, the "secrets" that make up the three secrets empow-erment are:

1. Gesture

2. Vocalization

3. Visualization/expectation

While the term "three secrets empowerment" comes from the Tibetan Black Hat school of feng shui, the actual practice is common to all, or at least most, magical traditions. In magical housekeeping, the three secrets empowerment is used to magically imbue objects, placements, and enhancements with the magnetic power of your intentions.

Know What You Want

First, clarify and record your intention. For example, let's say you've just added a romantic statue to your love and marriage corner, and you'd like to empower it with the intention to invite a serious love relationship into your life. So, to clarify and record your intention, you would write in the present tense (as if it were already true) exactly what you'd like to manifest, possibly something like: "I now experience a passionate and satisfying love relationship with a partner who challenges and supports me in all the most perfect ways." (Important note: in this case, you would want to leave the identity of this person up to the universe. This is because it's not ethical to metaphysically manipulate others, and the outcome will be much better this way.) You can also empower whole rooms or areas, or even the entire house, with the three secrets empowerment. For example, you could choose to empower your gratitude and prosperity area with the following intention: "I constantly receive abundance from an Infinite Source," or you could choose to empower your entire house with the intention that "Peace, harmony, and happiness are now powerfully established within these walls." I also like to empower my front door with this intention: "I now invite health, wealth, happiness, gratitude, and love to flow into my life in abundance." There is really no end to what you can do with the three secrets.

Now that you've clarified your intention and decided what you'd like to empower, you can select a gesture and vocalization to go along with the intention. Below, you'll find a useful assortment of gestures and vocalizations from a number of different traditions. If you're an experienced magical practitioner or practice gesture and vocalization from a different practice or tradition (such as yoga), feel free to choose gestures and vocalizations from your own personal toolbox. As you go through the choosing process, you can try out the gestures and vocalizations to see if they feel powerful for you. Once you've chosen, write down your selections below your intention so that you have them all in one place before I explain how to put them all together, which I promise I will do shortly.

Gestures

Prayer Pose

Hands gently pressing into each other at the heart, palms and fingers flat, fingers pointing up.

> **Good for:** manifestation, balance, calm power,
> enlisting the help of the Divine and your higher self

This is a good all-purpose gesture and is present in many traditions.

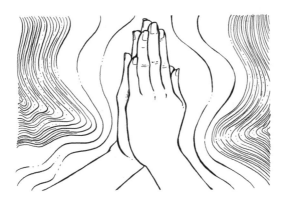

Blessing Mudra

Palms up, pinky edge of palms touching. Little fingers crossed with thumbs holding down tips of little fingers. Ring fingers side by side, pointing up. Middle fingers crossed, index fingers holding down tips of middle fingers.

> **Good for:** manifestation, protection, balance, synchronicity, divine support in all matters

Expelling Mudra

Palms down, hold ring and middle finger under thumbs, index and pinky extended. Repeatedly flick ring and middle fingers.

> **Good for:** removing obstacles, banishing, paving the way for success

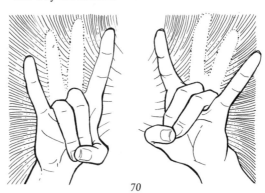

Heart-Calming Mudra

Hands lightly cupped, left hand over the right, fingers of the left hand pointing right and fingers of the right hand pointing left, tips of thumbs lightly touching.

> **Good for:** serenity, clarity, harmony, joyful awareness

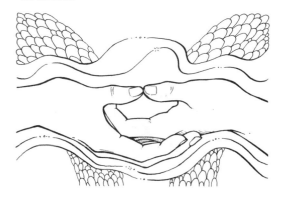

Guyan Mudra

Palms up, upper arms resting against body, forearms extended out and 45 degrees up on each side, thumb and forefinger of each hand touching, other fingers extended straight and together.

> **Good for:** receptivity, calm personal power

Active Guyan Mudra

Like guyan mudra, but with the forefingers curled under the thumbs.

> **Good for:** active power, calm authority, confidence

Buddhi Mudra

Like guyan mudra, but with the thumb touching the little finger instead of the forefinger.

> **Good for:** harmonious communication and connections with others in both the seen and the unseen worlds

Jupiter Mudra

Fingers interlaced, thumbs crossed, forefingers extended straight and touching.

> **Good for:** focus, confidence, overcoming obstacles, dissolving barriers

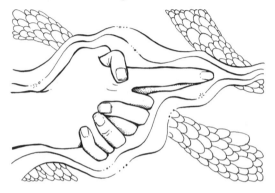

Goddess Posture

Feet hip-distance apart, arms extended up like a V, fingers straight and together, palms facing in and up, so that your hands are extensions of the line of your arms.

> **Good for:** invoking and/or embodying divine feminine energy, calling on the Great Goddess in any of her many forms

God Posture

Ankles touching, hands in fists, hands crossed at chest, palms facing inward.

> **Good for:** invoking and/or embodying divine
> masculine energy, calling on God in any of his
> many forms

Cup Running Over

Create a cup with both hands, with the pinky edge of hands touching and palms facing up. Visualize and feel abundant blessings in the form of sparkly, golden-white light pouring down from above, filling your cupped hands, and running over.

> **Good for:** manifesting abundance, trusting that
> you are safe and provided for, learning to
> graciously receive

Reiki Mittens

Slightly cup hands individually and turn palms outward toward item or area you wish to empower, visualizing and feeling clear universal light with rainbow sparkles flowing in through the top of your head, down to your heart, and out through the palms of your hands.

> **Good for:** empowering objects or areas with
> universal light and love, which brings exactly
> what is needed for healing, manifestation,
> balance, and attunement with the Divine

Vocalizations

Once you've decided on your intention and your gesture, it's time to select a vocalization that goes along with them and feels powerful for you. Here are some ideas:

Affirmations and Rhymes

A very simple option would be to use your stated intention as your vocalization in affirmation form. In other words, say your intention is this: "I now experience a passionate and satisfying love relationship with a partner who challenges and supports me in all the most perfect ways." Because this is in the present form, as if it were already true, it's a perfectly constructed affirmation, and so you could very simply and effectively let your intention double as your vocalization.

Rhymes are very magical, and if rhyming feels especially powerful for you, this is also a good option. Using the above intention again as an example, you might compose a vocalization like: "One plus one is two, the love we share is true, our passion ever-new." A benefit of rhyming is that it brings a spirit of fun and playfulness, which opens doors of possibility and lends a whimsical quality to the magic and its effects.

Names for the Divine

You could also choose a divine name for your vocalization. Just by consciously speaking the name of a specific deity, you can invoke that deity and his/her accompanying qualities and powers. Here are some powerful deities whose names you might like to invoke for specific purposes. Of course, feel free to choose deities that are not on this list.

Forseti: The Norse god of fairness and justice. Forseti establishes fair, just, and swift resolution of disputes and legal matters.

Ganesh: The elephant-headed deity from the Hindu tradition. Ganesh offers very effective obstacle removal and paves the way for success.

Isis: A well-loved Egyptian goddess often shown with wings. Isis's gifts include feminine power and strength, balance and harmony with regard to responsibilities, and accomplishment balanced with relaxation and receptivity.

Krishna and Radha: The divine lovers from the Hindu tradition. Krishna and Radha infuse us with the energies of harmonious and passionate romantic love.

Lakshmi: The beautiful Hindu goddess of prosperity, often shown in or near a river and with elephants. Lakshmi can endow us with wealth, abundance, and luxury.

Maitreya: The rotund and happy Buddha you always see at Chinese restaurants. Maitreya's gifts include abundance, abiding joy, and trust in the Divine. He is also called Hotei, or Laughing Buddha.

Michael: The head archangel with the fiery sword. Michael brings powerful cleansing and protection, synchronicity, and confidence.

Quan Yin: The female counterpart to the Buddha. Quan Yin brings serenity, spirituality, purity, and gentle love.

Raphael: The archangel of air and the divine physician. Raphael helps with health and healing for the mind, body, and emotions.

Saint Martha: The Catholic saint often pictured with a dragon. Saint Martha offers harmony and happiness in the family and home.

Yemaya: The beautiful Yoruba goddess of the ocean and motherhood. Yemaya brings very deep alignment with your true self and true calling, helps with manifesting the deepest desires of your heart, and can help to gently and effectively cleanse away what no longer serves you or your purpose.

The Six True Words

The six true words are "Om ma ni pad me hum." This is a good all-purpose vocalization to choose, as it calls upon the universal love/light energy to heal, bless, and empower in the exact way(s) we most need it. It's untranslatable, and it's considered to be extremely powerful.

Aham Prema

Aham prema means "I am divine love." It opens and balances the heart center, harmonizes relationships, attracts true love, and increases both receptivity and generosity.

Ong So Hung

Ong so hung means "Creator, I am thou!" This is a good one to choose if you'd like to awaken the divine spark within in order to feel happy, healthy, powerful, and free, and to manifest any or all of the true desires of your heart.

Siri Gaitri Mantra

The siri gaitri mantra is "Ra ma da sa, sa say so hung." It calls upon the sun, moon, earth, and infinity, and brings them all together in the totality of your being. Choose this vocalization for healing on all levels, deep alignment with All That Is, harmony, balance, deeply rooted joy, and to activate and utilize the fullness of your magical power.

Guru Mantra

The guru mantra is "Wahe guru," and it is an untranslatable exclamation of wonder at the infinite, beautiful, and mysterious nature of the Divine. It opens doors of possibility and draws conditions with very high spiritual vibrations.

Putting It All Together
(1 Gesture + 1 Vocalization + 1 Visualization = The Three Secrets)

To perform the three secrets empowerment, it's important that you feel calm, clear, positive, and comfortable. For this reason, you might want to bathe first and slip into something comfortable. It's also important that the house is clean and clutter-free and that the energy has recently been cleansed.

Stand near the item or in the area you'd like to empower with your intention. Take some deep breaths and relax. Now begin to focus on your intention. Visualize and feel the feelings that go along with experiencing exactly what you'd like to experience. Now, hold the gesture, close your eyes, and, with confidence and strength in your voice, repeat the vocalization a predetermined number of times.* (Three and nine are popular and effective choices, but choose a number that feels right to you.) When you've finished the vocalization, with your eyes still closed, once again very powerfully visualize and feel that your intention has already manifested into form. For example, if it's your intention to manifest abundance, you might visualize yourself depositing huge checks into your bank account, going out to eat at your favorite restaurants, looking with joy at the ever-increasing balance on your bank statement, going on fun vacations, etc. Feel the feelings you'd like to feel when this occurs. You might also visualize wealth in the form of bright golden light filling and swirling around your home, your aura, and your wallet. As soon as the feelings and visualizations begin to fade, open your eyes and go about your day with total confidence that your empowerment was a success. And, just like when you delegate an important task to a highly trusted friend or family member, place complete trust in the Divine to perfectly assist you with this matter on every level.

Sample Empowerments

Here are a few sample empowerments I've assembled to give you an idea of how to plan your own. But, if you discover an empowerment below that resonates with you and fits your intention, go ahead and use it as is, or tweak it a little until it feels just right.

---

* I *do* recommend having a junk drawer, because there are some things that just don't seem to go anywhere else. Just make sure you clear it often.

Wealth & Abundance

Area/item to be empowered: The foyer (the area just inside the front door, where blessings enter the house)

Intention: "I constantly receive perfect abundance from the Infinite Source."

Gesture: Cup running over

Vocalization: "Lakshmi," repeated nine times (calling on the name of the goddess)

Visualization: Huge amounts of cash, coins, checks, gold, and sparkly golden light pouring down from above, flooding the entire body and aura, filling the room, and then moving powerfully throughout the rest of the house.

Harmonious Romance

Area/item to be empowered: A red, heart-shaped candle

Intention: "My partner and I now experience harmonious and passionate romance."

Gesture: Heart-calming mudra

Vocalization: "Aham prema." ("I am divine love.")

Visualization: See and/or feel yourself and your partner laughing together and feeling so happy, so loving, and so loved. See pink light surrounding and swirling around the two of you as you embrace, then mentally direct the same sparkly pink light into the candle. Now each time you light it, you'll be releasing this energy into your life and magnetizing your desired outcome.

Happiness & Joy

Area/item to be empowered: Every room of the house

Intention: "This home is filled with happiness and joy."

Gesture: Buddhi mudra

Vocalization: (same as intention) "This home is filled with happiness and joy."

Visualization: Laughter, smiles, the feeling of a happy heart, harmonious interactions, golden light filling each room with sparkles moving upward like champagne bubbles. Move to each room/area and repeat the empowerment.

6

Gemstones

FOR MANY CENTURIES and in many cultures, gemstones have been used to heal and bless. They have also been employed to manifest a number of wonderful things, including romance, abundance, happiness, serenity, and success. This chapter will introduce some helpful gemstones and their properties, and will explain how you can employ them in your magical housekeeping practice.

Cleansing Your Crystal

While you employ a crystal for a magical purpose, make sure you cleanse it on a regular basis, as it can absorb and hold negative vibrations. Do this at least once a week in one or more of the following ways:

- Set it in bright sunlight for at least a half-hour.
- Run it under cold tap water for at least one minute.
- Set it in a clean, moving body of water for at least one minute.
- Bury it in a dish of sea salt for at least twenty minutes.

- Smudge it with white sage smoke for as long as you feel it's necessary (usually not longer than one minute).

Placement

The simplest way to use a crystal in magical housekeeping is to place it in your environment. Begin by charging it with your intention, as described below.

Charging a Crystal with Your Intention

To charge a crystal with a specific intention, hold it in your open right hand, cupped slightly and cradled by your left hand. Close your eyes, focus on your intention as if it's already manifested, and visualize the energy of your manifested intention as bright white light that fills the crystal. Hold this intention for around thirty seconds, seeing and feeling the crystal pulsating and swirling with the light and energy of your intention.

Choosing a Placement

Depending on the crystal and your intention, you could place it a number of places, such as:

- Under your pillow or near your bed. In this placement, you'll absorb the energies of the crystal as you sleep.

- On an altar. Here, it will simultaneously represent your intention and help bring it into form. You can even create an altar around your specific intention, using the crystal as a focal point or enhancement.

- In a meditation area. This way, you can absorb the crystal's energies while you meditate, which will help you to receive insight, guidance, and healing specific to your intention.

- Other places specific to the crystal and intention. Ideas for placements are included in the crystal descriptions below.

Once you place the crystal, if you like, you can perform the three secrets empowerment to enhance the magic (see chapter 5).

Essences

Also known as gem elixirs, essences are the vibration of the crystal preserved in water and brandy. For our purposes, using a gemstone essence involves placing a few drops in a household cleaner or room spray in order to diffuse the vibration of the crystal throughout the room. You can purchase gemstone essences already made or make your own. The gemstone essences that can be purchased can also be taken internally, but if you make your own for use in your magical housekeeping practice (see below), I don't recommend that you take them internally unless you're an expert, or at least until you've done some more thorough research of gem essence preparation.

· ·

How to Create a Gem Essence

INGREDIENTS:

A cleansed crystal (you choose the type according to your needs—see below)

Pure water

A very clean, clear wine glass

Brandy

A small bottle with a dropper

On a sunny day, when the moon is between new and full, place the crystal in the glass. Pour the water over the crystal to fill the glass. Place the glass in bright sunlight for at least three hours, making sure that no shade hits it. During this time, set the empty dropper bottle next to the glass to purify it with the light of the sun. After the water and bottle have bathed in the sun for the allotted time, place your hands over the water and visualize very bright, sparkly light filling it. Say a quick prayer, like:

> *Great Spirit, please infuse this water with vibrations*
> *of healing and love. Please fully activate the*
> *positive energy of this crystal, and fill the water*
> *with it so that the water is powerful medicine and*
> *a helpful ally to me in my magical workings.*

Then fill the dropper bottle with half brandy, half water from the wineglass, using the dropper to transfer the water into the bottle. This will preserve the vibration of the crystal in the water.

Once you've made the essence, you can put four drops in a room spray or cleaning solution to diffuse the vibrations throughout the room. You can also put a few drops on your wrists, rubbing them together to internalize the magic and for personal healing.

The Crystals

There are many types of crystals with a huge array of unique healing properties. Below, I've included some that I've found especially helpful for magical housekeeping purposes. Use them in essence form, by placing them in the ways I've described above, or in any of the ways I've described below that are unique to each crystal. And feel free to try out other ones, too! (See bibliography for sources.)

Amethyst

Amethyst has a very deep and spiritual vibration. It aligns you with your higher self and universal consciousness. It helps you to see the Divine within everything and creates feelings of deep relaxation and inner harmony. Amethyst also replaces fear and worry with the trust that you're perfectly safe and perfectly provided for. Placing an amethyst under your pillow or near your bed will help you get a good night's sleep, as will misting your room with a room spray containing four drops of amethyst essence.

Bring this crystal into your space when:

- You'd like to alleviate depression and / or negativity.
- You're experiencing insomnia, anxiety, and / or stress.
- You'd like to manifest more abundance.
- You're suffering from an addiction.

In addition to the ideas mentioned at the beginning of the chapter, here are some good ways to use this crystal:

- Place in your gratitude and prosperity area to help manifest abundance by replacing worry with trust.
- Place in your synchronicity and miracles area to help align you with divine consciousness.
- Place in your serenity and self-love area to align you with deep spiritual vibrations.

Angelite

Aptly named, angelite has very high angelic vibrations. It helps bring coolness and receptivity to the emotions, which fosters harmonious communication. When you set the intention, angelite can also help hold the vibrations of the angelic realm within your space and your life. It's good for lifting you out of the illusions of lack and discord and into the perception of divine precision and the knowledge that all is well.

Bring this crystal into your space when:

- You'd like to bring the vibrations of the angelic realm into your home.

- You'd like to cool harsh emotions and create harmonious communication.

- You're ready to let go of the illusions of lack and discord and instead perceive the harmony and perfection in all.

In addition to the ideas mentioned at the beginning of the chapter, here are some good ways to use this crystal:

- Place it in your synchronicity and miracles area to align with the angelic realm and bring its vibrations into your home.

- Place it in your creativity and playfulness area to heal communication with your children and/or inner child.

- Place it in your creativity and playfulness area to help you express yourself in a spiritual and high vibratory way.

Apophyllite

Apophyllite, a clear crystal that forms in pyramids, cubes, and clusters, is very clear and bright, with rainbows and a sparkly, liquid, otherworldly, very highly vibrating energy. It's actually a physical representation of universal light. It lifts spirits; enhances imagination, intuition, and memory; helps connect you with other dimensions and realms (including the angelic and fairy realms); helps remove lingering traces of past physical and/or emotional dis-ease; and encourages flights of whimsical adventure.

Bring this crystal into your space when:

- You'd like to connect with other realms to receive healing, inspiration, and/or information.

- You'd like to enhance your creativity and imagination.

- You'd like to enhance your intuition.

- You'd like to enhance your memory.

- You're interested in releasing the final lingering traces of old emotional or physical hurts or traumas.

- You'd like to lift the vibrations of your space to a very high level.

- You'd like to call angels and/or fairies into your space.

In addition to the ideas mentioned at the beginning of the chapter, here are some good ways to use this crystal:

- Place it near your workspace to enhance your creativity, inspiration, intuition, and/or memory.

- Place it in your creativity and playfulness area to enhance your imagination and creativity.

- Place it in your synchronicity and miracles area to summon angels and/or fairies into your space and to connect you with universal light.

- Place it under your pillow to receive guidance and healing in your dreams and/or to visit other realms in your sleep.

Aqua Aura

This crystal is the love child of white quartz and gold. When treated at a very high temperature with gold, white quartz becomes a miraculous shade of aqua (hence the name). This crystal is my favorite. It's a stone of pure joy, contentment, confidence, self-knowledge, self-expression, and personal freedom. It imparts a buoyant, clear, and mystical vibration to mind, body, and spirit.

Bring this crystal into your space when:

- You'd like to elevate your consciousness to, and align your space with, fairy, angelic, and magical realms.

- You'd like to know yourself/love yourself/ express yourself more completely.

- You'd like to infuse your space with clear, joyful, and mystical vibrations.

- You'd like to raise your prosperity consciousness by thinking of money matters

as fun and adventurous rather than as a heavy
burden of responsibility.

- You could use a positive energy boost.

In addition to the ideas mentioned at the beginning of the
chapter, here are some good ways to use this crystal:

- Place it near your creative workspace to help
  you express your uniqueness.

- Place it in your creativity and playfulness area
  to activate the creative and whimsical energies
  associated with this area.

- Place it in your synchronicity and miracles area
  to enlist the assistance of fairies and angels in
  your life.

Aquamarine

Like a clear mountain stream, this crystal has a light, refresh-
ing, cooling, and purifying effect on the body, mind, and
emotions.

Bring this crystal into your space when:

- You could benefit from detoxification on the
  physical, emotional, and/or spiritual level.

- You'd like to experience more clarity.

- You'd like to experience gentle healing on any
  or every level.

- You feel you need to lighten up.

In addition to the ideas mentioned at the beginning of the
chapter, here are some good ways to use this crystal:

- Put it in your creativity and playfulness area to
  add lightness and joy to your life and to help

purify you of old emotional injuries or blocks
suffered by your inner child.

- Put it in your health and family relationships
area to help heal and purify old family issues
and detoxify your emotions and physical body.

Citrine Quartz

Citrine is an orange or yellow variety of quartz. It brings
pure sunshine, happiness, and general positive energy. Citrine
also helps with abundance on emotional, mental, and spiritual
levels. It can help you increase your conscious awareness of the
infinite nature of abundance and warm up to the idea of receiving abundance, which of course makes abundance more read-
ily available to you.

Bring this crystal into your space when:

- You'd like to shed some sunshiny energy into
your space and life.

- You'd like to consciously heal your attitudes
about wealth.

- You'd like to increase your financial prosperity.

In addition to the ideas mentioned at the beginning of the
chapter, here are some good ways to use this crystal:

- Place it in your serenity and self-love area to
help you cheer up and/or lighten up.

- Place it in your serenity and self-love area to
help heal your attitudes about wealth.

- Place it in your serenity and self-love area to
help increase your financial prosperity.

- Place it near your bill paying area, checkbook, and/or financial documents to help you with your attitude about managing your money, and therefore to help prosperity flow to you in a more abundant way.

Fluorite

Fluorite has a very fresh and clear energy. It works to alleviate stress by simplifying your conscious perceptions, organizing and clarifying thoughts, and bringing peace to the emotions. It also enhances self-love by assisting with the discovering and fostering of your own personal talents and abilities.

Bring this crystal into your space when:

- You feel emotionally or mentally overwhelmed.

- You've recently cleaned, cleared clutter, and/or organized, and you'd like to clear the energy left over from the clutter and confusion.

- You have trouble with decision making.

- You feel a lack of self-love due to a difficulty in recognizing your strengths.

- You're ready to discover or align more deeply with your unique talents and abilities.

In addition to the ideas mentioned at the beginning of the chapter, here are some good ways to use this crystal:

- Place it in your serenity and self-love area to help you discover and/or foster your unique talents and abilities.

- Place it in your serenity and self-love area to promote inner calm and serenity.

- Place it in your career and life path area to help align your career with your unique talents and abilities.

- Place it in your creativity and playfulness area to bring freshness and clarity to your creative outlook and / or projects.

- Place it near your workspace to promote clarity and to help you to see the simplest and most effective way to do any given thing (which helps with time management).

Garnet

Garnet ignites the emotions with a deep, long-burning passion and moves you into the realm of sensual perception and enjoyment. Both earthy and fiery in nature, it connects you with the true power that comes from fully inhabiting your body and fully owning and expressing your sexuality.

Bring garnet into your space when:

- You'd like to connect more fully with your body and sexuality.

- You'd like to bring more passion and physical enjoyment into a relationship.

- You'd like to manifest your hopes and dreams by grounding them in the physical realm and taking concrete steps toward them.

- You feel self-conscious about your body and / or appearance.

- You'd like to feel and appear sexier.

- You could use an extra dose of courage.

In addition to the ideas at the beginning of the chapter, here are some good ways to use this crystal:

- Place it in your love and marriage area to connect with your sensuality, self-love, and appreciation of your body.

- Place it in your love and marriage area to manifest a passionate love relationship or to enhance an already existing one.

- Place it in your radiance and reputation area to ignite your confidence and courage.

- Place it in your synergy, balance, and bliss area to help you manifest your hopes and dreams by grounding them in the physical realm.

- Place it in your synergy, balance, and bliss area to help you feel grounded and powerful.

Lapis Lazuli

Lapis is truly a gift. It brings feelings of pure joy and child-like bliss by making you aware that the everyday world of form is drenched in and inseparable from the magical worlds of all possibility. Lapis is very good medicine for children and inner children who have been forced to grow up early as a result of trauma. If you haven't given yourself time to play or permission to let your imagination wander and soar, this stone is for you. It's aligned with the infinite, mystical nature of the universe. Its qualities also help you align with your intuitive, magical, and psychic abilities.

Bring this crystal into your space when:

- Your energy or spirits have been lagging due to a lack of playfulness, joy, and flights of imagination.

- Your child is experiencing or healing from trauma.

- You're ready to heal old childhood issues.

- You'd like to bring feelings of pure, deep joy and freedom into your space.

- You'd like to align more deeply with your intuitive, magical, and psychic abilities.

In addition to the ideas mentioned at the beginning of the chapter, here are some good ways to use this crystal:

- Place it under your child's pillow or near your child's head while she sleeps, to help her experience the joy of childhood even during or after traumas.

- Place it in your creativity and playfulness area to encourage your inner child to play and imagine.

- Place it in your serenity and self-love area to help you align with your intuitive, magical, and psychic abilities.

- Place it near your creative workspace to strengthen and enhance creativity and add a magical, whimsical quality to your work.

Lepidolite

Lepidolite—sometimes pinkish, sometimes purplish; polished stones appear smooth, with silvery sparkles—brings lightness, joy, and sparkle to the heart and opens pathways to love and harmonious synchronicities. It has a radiant, playful, buoyant, fairylike energy that magnetizes both fairy energy and ideal romantic partners and conditions. It encourages self-love. It can also be very good for children who need help with confidence or are not playing enough.

Bring this crystal into your space when:

- You'd like to lighten up the atmosphere with sparkly, joyful vibrations.
- You'd like to attract fairies and fairylike energy to your space.
- You'd like to play and enjoy yourself more.
- You'd like to attract an ideal romantic partner or condition.
- You'd like to love yourself more.
- You'd like to open your heart to love.
- Your child's confidence or sense of play could use some bolstering.

In addition to the ideas mentioned at the beginning of this chapter, here are some good ways to use this crystal:

- Place it in your creativity and playfulness area to attract fairies, increase your playfulness, support your child, and/or enhance your creativity.
- Place it in your love and marriage area to attract an ideal partner or ideal romantic conditions.
- Place it in your love and marriage area to increase self-love and open your heart to love.
- Place it in your child's room to enhance his confidence and encourage playfulness.

Moonstone

Moonstone is pure receptivity. It's the softer, gentler side of things. It aligns you with lunar energy and the divine feminine.

Bring this crystal into your space when:

- You'd like to bring the soft, receptive energy of the moon into your space and life.
- You'd like to align yourself more deeply with your intuition.
- You're interested in strengthening your relationship with Goddess.
- You're in the process of healing your emotions.
- You'd like to increase your capacity to receive.
- You'd like to balance excess masculine energy with more feminine energy.
- You'd like to receive healing and support regarding feminine physical issues such as difficult menstruation or menopause.

In addition to the ideas mentioned at the beginning of this chapter, here are some good ways to use this crystal:

- Place it in your love and marriage area to increase your capacity to receive love and support.
- Place it in your love and marriage area to open yourself up to romantic possibilities.
- Place it in your creativity and playfulness or serenity and self-love area to increase your intuitive powers.

- Place it in your synchronicity and miracles
  area to invite the help of the moon and lunar
  goddesses into your life.

Moss Agate

Moss agate heals on a very deep level by relieving stress, strengthening the heart, and connecting you with the healing energy of the earth and plants. It has a very soothing and gently empowering energy. It also helps to bring harmony to families and family relationships.

Bring this crystal into your space when:

- You feel overwhelmed, overworked, and/or
  stressed.

- Your immune system could use a boost.

- You'd like to deepen your relationship with the
  earth and plants.

- You'd like to bring comforting and soothing
  energy into your environment.

- You'd like to bring harmony and healing to
  family relationships.

In addition to the ideas mentioned at the beginning of the chapter, here are some good ways to use this crystal:

- Place it in your health and family relationships
  area to strengthen your heart, health, and
  immune system.

- Place it in your health and family relationships
  area to strengthen and harmonize family
  relationships.

- Place it in your serenity and self-love area
  to soothe and revitalize an overwhelmed,
  overworked, or stressed-out mind.

- Place it in your synchronicity and miracles area
  to align yourself with, and receive help and
  guidance from, plants and the earth.

Important note: Don't place it in the place you are when you experience stress and strain, such as your workspace, because moss agate revitalizes and restores rather than counterbalances. Instead, use either fluorite to create clarity or obsidian to absorb harsh and negative vibrations. Then use the moss agate later, when you're out of the area.

Obsidian

Obsidian has an amazingly ancient and wise energy. Its ability to absorb negativity is legendary. Because of this quality, it must be cleansed often to release and purify it of these energies. If there's an area that often or sometimes becomes charged with negative, intense, and/or excessive energy, obsidian can help neutralize this energy and create a clearer, gentler, more serene atmosphere. Because its energy is so deep and soothing, it can also help align you with your true purpose and career path, especially when you've been experiencing tension and worry about the subject.

Bring this crystal into your space when:

- You'd like to create clarity and serenity by
  neutralizing the effects of harsh emotions or
  events.

- You'd like to reduce the occurrence of discord,
  unkind words, and/or hurt feelings in your
  space.

- You'd like to create a calmer atmosphere by
drawing off the effects of excess energy and
anxiety.

In addition to the ideas at the beginning of the chapter, here
are some good ways to use this crystal:

- Place it in any area where you tend to
experience harshness, discord, excess energy,
and/or anxiety.

- Place it in your career and life path area to help
you align with your true purpose and career
path.

- Place it in your serenity and self-love area to
help you experience a deep sense of inner
stillness and calm.

Rose Quartz

Rose quartz has a very soft, loving, healing, relaxing, soothing, heart-opening vibration. It helps you rest, enhances
romance, creates harmony, and speeds healing on all levels.

Bring this crystal into your space when:

- You'd like to create a soothing atmosphere and
relieve stress.

- You'd like to experience more harmony and
sweetness in your life.

- You'd like to experience more harmony and
sweetness in your love life.

- You'd like to enhance healing on any level.

In addition to the ideas mentioned at the beginning of the
chapter, here are some good ways to use this crystal:

- Put two, side by side, in your love and marriage area or bedroom to help manifest a romantic relationship or harmonize an existing one.

- Place it under or near your pillow for healing and to help you sleep comfortably and soundly.

- Place it in your serenity and self-love area to help relieve stress and enhance self-love.

- If your child is especially sensitive, place it near her pillow to help heal and restore her physical and energetic bodies while she sleeps.

- Place it in your workspace to help soften and dispel harshness and/or negativity.

Rutilated Quartz

This crystal is made up of quartz filled with straight filaments of metallic rutile. It powerfully sorts out and heals abundance and self-esteem issues by bringing clarity, true wisdom, dynamic motivation, consciousness of your own power, and awareness of the infinite nature of your source. Like all quartz, it increases energy and focuses/directs intentions.

Bring this crystal into your space when:

- You'd like to feel more confident.

- You'd like to actively manifest abundance in the best possible way.

- You could use some courage, energy, wisdom, and/or motivation.

In addition to the ideas mentioned at the beginning of the chapter, here are some good ways to use this crystal:

- Place it in your gratitude and prosperity area to help motivate you, encourage you, and inspire you to manifest abundance.

- Place it in your workspace to keep you clear, focused, and inspired.

- Place it in your creativity and playfulness area to empower your creative endeavors and motivate you to proceed with your creative career.

- Place it in your serenity and self-love area to help you establish and/or stick to an exercise, diet, or meditation habit.

- Place it in your serenity and self-love area to help you experience success in your studies.

White/Clear Quartz

White/clear quartz purifies and amplifies. It's especially adept at holding the intention with which it's charged and directing it toward the manifestation of the desired outcome.

Bring this crystal into your space when:

- You'd like to amplify the energy already present in an item or area.

- You'd like to increase your physical, mental, and/or spiritual energy.

- You'd like to hold high and pure vibrations within an area.

- You'd like to clarify and direct a specific intention.

In addition to the ideas mentioned at the beginning of this chapter, here are some good ways to use this crystal:

- Place it in the power center of your home that corresponds with a specific intention (prosperity, career, health, etc.) on top of a piece of paper stating your intention as if it has already occurred.

- Place it with another crystal in order to amplify its power.

- Place it with another magical item (plant, image, etc.) in order to intensify its power.

- Place it in any area where you'd like to hold high and pure vibrations.

- Place it in any area where you'd like to experience more energy.

- Place it in your synchronicity and miracles area, creativity and playfulness area, serenity and self-love area, or career and life path area to amplify the energies associated with the area itself.

7

Fairies, Angels & Other Helpful Beings

I LOVE ENLISTING the help of divine and otherworldly beings. They're not only wonderfully helpful, but they also possess unique and delightful qualities that make them fun to get to know and hang around with. Many of them will just show up anytime you call on them (angels, for example), but some of them are a little more elusive (yes, fairies, this means YOU). In this chapter, I'm pleased to introduce you to some beings that I love to work with in my home, and give you some ideas for how you can work with them as well.

A Word about Altars

You probably won't want to assemble an altar for every single deity or group of deities that you work with in your home. In fact, you might never feel the need to assemble an altar at all. However, occasionally you might, as assembling and tending to an altar is a very powerful and effective magical act.

Assembling an Altar

An altar is an artful assembly of purposefully chosen sacred objects. It can be on a shelf, table, desktop, or any other surface. You can create an altar for a specific purpose or intention, such as manifesting wealth or enhancing your marriage, or you can create an altar to call in a specific deity, being, or group of beings. Either way, I suggest adding a picture or statue of a magical being or beings as a focal point, to bring the altar to life and enlist the patronage of the being(s) and/or call them into your space. A piece of cloth or a scarf is often a good addition to use as a base (table cloth) for your altar. I like to add a candle or candles to bring the altar to life, and incense or essential oils in an oil burner as a fragrant offering to the patron being(s) of the altar.

Other items you might like to place on your altar include crystals, flowers, fruit, affirmations, prayers, plants, dried herbs, or any other items that are significant to your goal or to the deity or deities. If you choose to place fruit or herbs on the altar, consider them offerings to the patron(s) of the altar, and do not consume them. When it's time to dispose of them, place them in a compost pile, bury them in the earth, or place them at the base of a tree; if none of these are possible, at the very least place them in the yard waste container so that they can be returned to the earth.

Tend to your altar regularly to keep its magic alive. Dust it, replace candles, add new items, and rearrange it as you feel guided. You can also lend strength to its magic with prayers, visualizations, and/or the three secrets empowerment.

A General Calling-In of Good Spirits

After cleansing the energy in your home (see chapter 3), it's always nice to invite sweet and helpful spirits into your space. This is a ritual that will help you do just that. Because it has to do with inviting spirits from the other side (spirit guides, helpful deceased loved ones, etc.), this ritual is best done at night. To begin, obtain a sweetgrass braid (a form of smudge stick or dried herb bundle, burned like incense) or a stick of sweetgrass or copal incense. Light a white or off-white candle, and bring your hands together near your heart in prayer pose. Close your eyes and take some deep breaths while consciously relaxing and tuning in to the subtle energetic realm and what is known as the otherworld. When you feel ready, light the braid or incense and say:

> *Sweet spirits of the otherworld, I call you.*
> *Divine beings of light, I invite you. You are*
> *welcome here. Reside, abide, dwell, and bless us*
> *(me) with your presence in our (my) home.*

Carry the smoking wand from room to room, being very aware of fire safety while continuing to summon sweet spirits, either mentally or aloud. When you're finished, give thanks to the beings you've summoned for answering your call, and extinguish the bundle or incense and candle. You'll find that after you do this, your home is filled with remarkable feelings of sweetness, light, comfort, and joy.

Angels

Angels are present in abundance and absolutely *adore* helping us. Their energy is very high, clear, bright, and nonjudgmental. They powerfully help with *everything*, especially safety, travel, synchronicity, miracles, healing, protection, and guidance. Calling angels into your space is always a good idea. To do this, you can just say (mentally or aloud) something like: "Angels, I call on you! Please fill this home with your bright light and your love." You can also call on them for more specific purposes.

Every day, after clearing the space in my home with a quick visualization (see chapter 3), I call on angels to surround it, directing positive energy inward and holding a very high vibration in the space. Then, I call on more angels to surround those angels, facing outward in order to protect my home and direct all negativity back to where it came from. I then visualize this happening. This always makes me feel totally safe, relaxed, and positive that my home is powerfully protected. I call this my simple angel protection ritual, and I go into it in more detail in chapter 11.

Artistic renderings of angels bring their energy into your home and help to hold it in place. Once you place your statue or hang your picture, do the three secrets empowerment to call angels into your space. An especially good place for pictures and/or statues of angels is your synchronicity and miracles area, as the energy of this area is totally in alignment with angelic assistance and guidance.

In addition to one or more pictures and/or statues of angels, some items you might choose for an angel altar include:

- White, gold, silver, and light blue (for the cloth and candles)

- Angelite, aqua aura, and apophyllite crystals

- Actual silver and gold

- Naturally shed white feathers

- Frankincense, lavender, or rose oil or incense

- Fresh flowers, especially lavender, roses, and camellias

Archangel Michael

The archangels are the superstars of the angelic hierarchy, and Michael is the archangels' archangel. He has a powerfully cleansing, bright, fiery energy. His sword of light removes heaviness, darkness, and negativity by quickly incinerating it and thereby transmuting it into positive energy. Personally, I work with Archangel Michael more than any other deity, as he's a "get things done" kind of guy, and with his swift ability to cleanse away negativity and create the most positive atmosphere possible, he is a man (or angel, to be more precise) after my own heart.

I'm very fond of performing this prayer/visualization (inspired by the work of Doreen Virtue—see bibliography) to enlist Michael's help to cleanse the energy of my home:

> *Sit comfortably and close your eyes. Ask Archangel*
> *Michael to powerfully fill your entire home with very*
> *bright white light. See him doing this, and see the*
> *white light pouring out from his hands and creating*
> *a giant bubble of light that completely envelops your*

home, extending outside its walls, above the roof, and below the earth like a giant energy field. Then, ask Michael to powerfully sweep away any lingering dark or negative spots within the energy field, and see or sense him doing this. You might like to imagine that he has a giant glowing vacuum tube that swiftly vacuums up this energy. Finish by calling on angels to surround your house, holding this positive energy in place.

In addition to one or more pictures/statues of Michael, some items you might choose for an altar devoted to Archangel Michael include:

- Royal blue or indigo (for cloth and candles)
- One or more candles are a must, as Michael's energy is so fiery
- Cedar, cinnamon, and frankincense oil or incense

Buddha

The Buddha, in his serenely meditating form, creates sacred space and confers feelings of deep stillness and clarity.

Placing a meditating stone Buddha near the outside of your front door purifies the energy that enters your home. In this placement, the Buddha also encourages all who enter to leave their earthly stressors and concerns at the door.

In your serenity and self-love area, a meditating Buddha statue helps you to stay grounded, centered, and calmly energized in your daily activities, which greatly benefits all areas of life.

The Buddha prefers simplicity. A good altar to him would include a picture or statue of him and one other item, such as a crystal or an incense burner.

The Divine Lovers (Krishna/Radha)

I'm very big on romance. I believe that everyone can benefit from romantic energy, even those who don't feel ready or willing to manifest a relationship. Krishna and Radha represent the interaction of the masculine and feminine energies in all things and the harmonious balance, raging success, and pure creativity that result from this merging.

In order to experience the dance of life to the fullest, it's important to strike a balance between masculine and feminine energies in your life. (This is true regardless of your sexual preference.) You must be able to balance the extremes: receiving/giving, yielding/standing firm, and resting/acting. This is necessary in order to manifest and experience a harmonious and passionate love relationship as well. Krishna and Radha can help with this; it's their specialty.

Pictures and statues of, or altars to, Krishna and Radha are excellent in the bedroom and love and marriage area to help create or manifest an ideal love relationship. In the serenity and self-love area, they help work on the internal level to balance the masculine and feminine energies within you. In the synchronicity and miracles area, they help you to be in the right place at the right time to meet your beloved. In the gratitude and prosperity area, they help you and your partner to heal and harmonize any money issues that have been coming between you, and they also help you both to manifest abundance in the best possible ways. (They might also help you attract a wealthy partner!)

In addition to an image or statue representing Krishna and Radha, some items you might choose for an altar devoted to them include:

- Temple and Nag Champa incense
- Rose and jasmine incense or oil
- Pink and red for candles and cloth
- Accents of orange, blue, and yellow for candles and cloth (as long as they are in addition to pink and/or red)
- Roses
- Jasmine
- Daisies
- Rose quartz hearts
- A flute
- A picture of you and your current partner

The Krishna and Radha Doorknob Charm for Passionate Romance

If you're ready to spice up your love life in a serious way, I suggest calling upon Krishna and Radha's assistance to create this powerful charm.

INGREDIENTS:

Fuschia or hot pink felt or cotton wool (something that doesn't unravel at the edges)

Red lace

Dried damiana (an herb)

Dried red rose petals

A small picture of Krishna and Radha
  (printed out from the Internet is fine)

Needle and thread

Essential oil of ylang ylang

A red candle

Anytime between the morning of the first day of the second quarter moon and midnight on the evening of the full moon, assemble the ingredients and light the candle. Cut two hearts roughly the size of your hand out of the fabric. Sew them into a small pillow, leaving an opening at the top or side. Lightly stuff the pillow with the damiana and rose petals. Then tuck the picture of Krishna and Radha inside as well. Sew the opening closed, and sew the ends of the lace on in such a way that the charm can neatly hang on your bedroom doorknob. (If you're the crafty type, you can also decorate the charm with lace in other ways too, like an old-fashioned valentine.) Put a dab of ylang ylang on the charm and hold it between your hands. Close your eyes and say a simple invocation and prayer to Krishna and Radha, such as:

> *Krishna and Radha, I call on you. I now choose to*
> *invite passionate romance into my life, and I ask for*
> *your divine assistance with this matter. Thank you.*

Hang the charm on the outside of your bedroom doorknob. Periodically, anoint it again with a bit of ylang ylang oil to keep the scent fresh. And then get ready: there is going to be some serious spiciness going on.

Fairies

Fairies are a lot of fun to live with. Their energy is earthy, whimsical, mischievous, adventurous, and joyful. They can help connect you with a spirit of playfulness and fun and can help your inner child and actual child or children to feel happy and loved. They can also help heal and protect your animal companions.

There are a lot of ways to call fairies into your home and garden, but fairies are fickle and have a few conditions first. Rule number one: do not use chemical pesticides in your home or garden if you want to attract fairies. Instead, for your home, consider using essential oils such as lemongrass and lavender, and for your garden, consider bringing in live ladybugs or consulting a permaculture book or website to see what creature or plant you might introduce to your garden in order to balance your unwanted bug population. Fairies will also be less likely to come around if you're not doing your personal best to protect and heal the environment and animals, as they are the guardians and divine manifestations of the natural world.

Artistic renderings of fairies in your home and/or garden can help summon them, especially when you place the statue or picture with the intention to invite them in. Inside your home, the creativity and playfulness area would be an especially good place for this. And remember to strengthen your intention to invite in the fairies by empowering your statue or picture with the three secrets.

Fairies enjoy the scent of jasmine. Burning jasmine oil in a burner is a good way to entice them to visit. They also like cinnamon incense.

As creatures of nature, fairies like all plants, but there are a few that they especially love to hang around, including primrose, jasmine, any blossoms that look like little bells, lavender, rosemary, sage, and all types of fruit blossoms. To invite fairies indoors, live potted plants are a must.

Fairies like shiny and sparkly things and things that move, like mobiles, flags, and wind chimes. They also like it when you leave offerings of bittersweet chocolate chips or little thimbles or walnut shell halves filled with beer, champagne, or sparkling cider. Any of these items will help entice fairies to come live with you. (*Note:* Whether your consumable gifts disappear or linger, be assured that the fairies—if they have chosen to grace you with their presence—have duly noted the gifts and the giver. If the gifts remain on the physical plane, it is quite possible that the fairies have still ingested the energetic essence of the gift. In other words, don't worry about putting the gifts in the compost heap before they start to mold.)

You might not see the fairies with your eyes, but if you're sensitive, you'll feel their presence. You'll likely feel feelings of giddiness, adventurousness, mischief, and an indescribable sort of pleasant wonder at the mystery of existence. Colors might also appear more vivid, and the movement of sunlight through the trees might seem more sparkly or luminous.

In addition to one or more pictures/statues of fairies, some items you might choose for a fairy altar include:

- Bells
- Shiny and sparkly things
- Jasmine and cinnamon oil or incense
- Fresh flowers

- Nature items such as pinecones, acorns, and feathers

- Sweets

- Fruit

- Aqua aura or apophyllite crystals

Springtime Fairy Invitation

Spring is an especially good time to invite the fairies to live in your home or garden. It's a time when they're especially festive and adventurous and are more in the mood to make their presence known to humans. Or maybe it's that we humans are more in the mood to commune with fairies in the springtime. Either way, it seems that spring is a time when the mists between the worlds of human and fairy are less substantial and easier to penetrate. And so, if it's spring and you feel that fairy fever is upon you, here's a way to invite the sparkling and uplifting presence of the fairies into your garden, home, and life.

INGREDIENTS:

Dried dill weed

8 walnut shell halves

1 bottle of good beer or sparkling cider

A white quartz crystal cluster

Fairies love to dance together around a circle under the full moon. At night, when the moon is full, in your yard or on your deck, use the dill weed to create an outline of a small circle (a little bigger than a large dinner plate). In the center of the circle, place the crystal. Around the outside of the circle, arrange the walnut shell halves and fill them with beer or cider. You've now set up an ideal fairy party site. Mentally or aloud, announce your invitation to the fairies. Say something like, "Fairies, I invite you to dance in my yard, and stay a while!" But be careful that you *don't* say thank you at any time when addressing the fairies, as it's said that fairies aren't too crazy about being thanked. All the items used for this invitation are natural, so I suggest that you leave them in your yard as a gift to the fairies. After your invitation, when you're in your yard, tune in to your intuition and see if you can sense the presence of fairies. You might want to repeat this one a few times, or wait a while and repeat. Fairies are a bit fickle, and for one reason or another might not come the first time they're invited. But if you earnestly desire their company, keep at it, and they will eventually accept. Once you establish a relationship with the fairies, you can ask them for help with various things, such as romance, happiness, abundance, and luck. Just make sure you offer them something for their trouble, like chocolate, beer, or crystals. Fairies are wonderful allies, but they aren't too keen on doing something for nothing.

Ganesh

Ganesh is the beloved elephant-headed deity from the Hindu tradition. He's so beloved because he's such a swift and powerful obstacle remover. He can clear the energetic pathway and remove any barriers or blocks so that you have the greatest possible chance of success in any and all areas and endeavors. When you call on him, you'll feel his energy arrive like a wrecking ball, helping to knock down what is standing between you and your ideal life situation. (This, incidentally, can be very helpful in the removal of clutter, as clutter is the physical manifestation of all forms of obstacles.)

If any area of your life feels stuck, place a statue of Ganesh in your synchronicity and miracles area and perform the three secrets empowerment with the intention to replace your experience of "stuck-ness" with free-flowing success. This cure can help effectively remove creative, financial, career, relationship, physical, or emotional blocks and get you moving in the right direction.

I've found that the type of altar that works best with Ganesh's no-nonsense energy is a simple one made up of three items: a Ganesh statue, a candle, and an incense burner. Types of incense that would be especially appropriate to burn to Ganesh would be Nag Champa, sage, copal, cinnamon, and frankincense.

Green Tara, the Goddess of Swift Compassion

Green Tara is a compassionate, green, usually bare-breasted mother goddess of the Tibetan tradition, and she can quickly help overcome fear and inertia, which, for one thing, can make the clutter-clearing process easier and more pleasant. She can also help with renovations, repairs, cleaning, and other projects. In short, if you're feeling overwhelmed with any aspect of your home or life, Tara will swiftly come to your rescue. Statues or pictures of her would be good in the synchronicity and miracles, radiance and reputation, or serenity and self-love areas. She's another that does well with a simple altar, such as a statue or picture, incense, and possibly a green candle or two.

Hestia

Hestia, Greek goddess of the hearth, brings feelings of warmth, safety, and harmony to the home. The hearth of a home is like the heart of a person. If there's a feeling of coldness or discord in your home, or if you have somehow never felt truly at home there, Hestia can help by opening and warming your home's heart. She can also help heal household disputes and confer a deep sense of general harmony and well-being. To call Hestia into your home, try the ritual below.

Hestia Invocation Ritual to Warm the Heart of the Home

Begin by designating your home's hearth, or heart. This will likely be your fireplace or your oven. It could also be a fireplace-type area such as a mantel that resembles a fireplace, or another central or often-used location where you can evoke hearth-like feelings by placing, say, a framed picture of a fireplace or one of those lights with blowing shredded fabric that gives the illusion of fire burning. Your intuition should give you a nudge, but if you can't decide between a few areas, consider choosing the one that's closest to the center of your home. You might also consider choosing the one that the members of the household tend to congregate around the most.

Once you've designated your hearth, place a large (perhaps multiple-wicked) orange or red-orange candle (ideally soy or vegetable wax) on or near it. Next to the candle, place a stick of cinnamon incense. Light both and say this invocation:

> *Hestia, I call on you! Please heal, open, and warm*
> *the heart of this home and bring it to life. Please*
> *fill this space, our hearts, and this household with*
> *happiness and harmony. Please sustain our spirits*
> *with an abundance of all wonderful things. Thank*
> *you, thank you, thank you. Blessed be. And so it is.*

Allow the candle to burn for at least one hour. You can allow it to burn all the way down, or extinguish and relight it on future occasions as convenient and desired. (You might also want to replace the candle once it burns out to keep the magic fresh.) Allow the incense to burn until it goes out naturally and light additional sticks as desired.

Kali, the Goddess of Destruction

Calling on Kali is like bringing in the big guns. She's the dark goddess of the Hindu tradition, capable of complete destruction and annihilation, like a hurricane or a wildfire. If you need help letting go of the old or are in need of some exceptionally powerful purification and release, Kali is the goddess for you. Kali might be especially helpful in situations where you've felt powerless for some time and are ready to reclaim your power by releasing old relationships, habits, and/or thought patterns.

I enlisted Kali's help with great success a few years back, when I was going through a particularly challenging time. I don't know if this has ever happened to you, but it was like my mind (ego) just wouldn't shut up, and all it was doing was criticizing me in a million different ways. "You are so pathetic," it would say. "Your new haircut looks terrible. You should be more successful by now, shouldn't you? What did you just say? What a stupid thing to say ... " and so on. And it was a trap! I would try to stop, and it would say, "Yeah, you really should be thinking more positive thoughts, shouldn't you? What's your problem? You've been reading self-help books for centuries, shouldn't you have mastered the art of positive thinking by now?" It was incessant. It seemed no matter what I tried, I found myself back in the trap. And it continued until I discovered how much Kali could help in situations like this! Whenever I noticed my thoughts beginning to run out of control with negativity, I just called on Kali by saying mentally "Kali! Help!" And boy did she stop my negative thought patterns in their tracks. I felt her liberating energy as a rush of power in my body, and mentally, I felt that I could simply step right out of my downward spiral and be free. It took some time to completely break the habit of negative thinking, as my mind kept going back to its old ways, but each time I called on Kali and stepped out of the cycle, it got easier and easier, until eventually I broke the habit.

Kali also helps with extreme clutter clearing, renovating, moving, and space clearing. I don't recommend having pictures or statues of Kali in your home permanently (unless she's a patron of yours or you could use some serious, long-term help with purification, ego eradication, and/or letting go), but I do suggest bringing her in during times of intense transition, when you're releasing the old to make room for the new. Good places for her would be the synchronicity and miracles, radiance and reputation, and serenity and self-love areas. An altar to Kali isn't necessary, as extra items are definitely not her cup of tea. Just her image and an extremely simple invocation will do the trick. If you'd like to enlist Kali's help for a specific purpose, you might try the following invocation:

. . . .

Kali Purification Invocation

Bring a statue or picture of Kali into your space. Choose an image that feels powerful and attractive to you, even if it feels a tiny bit frightening. (Because she's got such a fierce personality, it's natural that she might seem a little intimidating. But rest assured that when you call on her, she'll be your loyal ally, and she won't turn her destructive energy on anything other than that which no longer serves you.)

Stand in front of the image, close your eyes, and hold your hands in prayer pose. Focus on the situation, thought pattern, habit, or physical clutter that you'd like to purify or release. Open your eyes and do the expelling mudra (see page 70) forty times. Then, place your hands in prayer pose once more and gaze at the image as you say:

> *Kali, I call on you. Please destroy, dissolve,*
> *and completely annihilate all conditions and*
> *beliefs that no longer serve me, so that I may*
> *make room for the new. Thank you.*

Lakshmi

Lakshmi is the beautiful Hindu goddess of abundance. She's the divine expert on manifesting luxury and wealth. She helps us experience prosperity by showing us that we are infinitely deserving of the unending supply of money and resources that is always available to us.

Having a picture or statue of Lakshmi in your gratitude and prosperity area is a wonderful way to experience her presence and call increased abundance into your life. Empower it with the three secrets when you place it and periodically during the waxing or full moon.

You can also place a picture or statue of Lakshmi in your serenity and self-love area if you believe that you are undeserving of, or feel guilty about, experiencing wealth and luxury.

In addition to an image or statue representing Lakshmi, some items you might choose for an altar devoted to her include:

- Red, pink, and yellow roses and rose petals
- Red, pink, blue, and yellow for candles and cloth
- Metallic gold-colored items or actual gold
- A small fountain
- A picture or small statue/figurine of one or two elephants
- A dish or bowl of coins and/or paper money
- Nag Champa incense
- Jasmine incense or oil

Nemetona

Nemetona is the Celtic goddess of sacred groves. She has a very deep and mystical presence that encourages feelings of reverence and devotion. She's an excellent helper to call upon to bring very high spiritual vibrations to your space. I like to call on her to help with space clearing and to set the tone for my meditation area. She's especially fond of the outdoors, so she's also good to call on to bless and consecrate your outdoor areas.

Pictures and statues of Nemetona are not common, so if you feel drawn to create an altar to Nemetona, or to bring her image into your space, light a candle and say a prayer to her, asking her to present you with the perfect image to represent her and summon her energy. Then surrender the situation to God/Goddess/All That Is and follow any intuitive hunches you might have. She's most commonly imagined as a dark-haired beauty with a cloak, standing outside at night near a grove of trees.

In addition to an image representing Nemetona, some items you might choose for an altar devoted to her include:

- Deep blue, black, forest green, cream, and white (for candles and cloth)
- An unlit bundle of sage
- Leaves
- Obsidian, white quartz, and moss agate
- Cedar incense
- Nag Champa incense

Calling on Nemetona is best done after dark. To create sacred space and invite a feeling of deep reverence and spiritual devotion in your home, I suggest trying out the following invocation:

. . . .

Nemetona Sacred Oak Invocation

During the full moon, light a blue candle. Hold your hands in prayer pose and say:

> *Nemetona, I call on you! I invite you to dwell in*
> *this home. Please protect it in all ways. Please*
> *preserve its deep mystery and magic, and fill it*
> *with vibrations of reverence and awe. Thank you,*
> *thank you, thank you. Blessed be. And so it is.*

Now feel her presence and energy in the space. You might see her bringing in her energy as sparkly starlight descending from the night sky and golden white light rising up from the earth, swirling together beautifully and moving gracefully throughout the space. Once this light fills the entire space, ask Nemetona to anchor it in place with a huge oak tree made of white light. Visualize the trunk of this massive tree being so large that it contains and encompasses your entire house and the area immediately around it. Then see the roots of this tree descend deep into the earth and its branches extend high into the sky.

St. Francis of Assisi

Saint Francis is a very gentle, peaceful, and loving saint. His presence in your home can help simplify your life and create vibrations of serenity, calm wisdom, and connection with nature and All That Is. I also like to call on him with a simple prayer to protect and look after my very beloved cats.

One way to align with Saint Francis's energy would be to place a picture or statue of him in your home. An especially good place for this would be your serenity and self-love area. You could then do the three secrets empowerment to call him in and/or enlist him for help with a certain issue, such as creating simplicity and serenity or protecting your companion animals. If you call him in specifically to watch over your animals, other good places for him would be the synchronicity and miracles area or the creativity and playfulness area.

In addition to one or more pictures of Saint Francis, some items you might choose for an altar devoted to him include:

- Whole, unshelled nuts such as chestnuts and walnuts
- Leaves from trees, pinecones, and acorns
- A bowl or dish of dried yarrow and/or oatgrass
- A simple wooden Catholic rosary
- A wooden cross

- White, tan, and brown (for cloth and candles)
- A picture or pictures of your companion animal(s)
- Naturally shed feathers, whiskers, claws, or baby teeth from your companion animal or another animal
- Live plants
- Juniper, cedar, and sweetgrass incense or oil

. . . .

Saint Francis Companion Animal Protection Invocation

Place a white or off-white candle next to a statue or image of Saint Francis and light it. Sit or stand with your spine straight, hold your hands in prayer pose, and relax. Now, enlist his gentle yet powerful support in protecting your beloved companion animal(s) by saying:

> *Saint Francis, I call on you to protect my beloved companion animal(s), _____. Please watch over him (her/them) at all times, and keep him safe. Please keep him company while I am away. Please nurture him, uplift his spirits, and infuse his heart with joy. Please always bring him safely home to me. Thank you, thank you, thank you. Blessed be. And so it is.*

When you're finished with the invocation, to express your gratitude to Saint Francis for protecting your companion(s), decide on, and commit to, one small (or large) action or lifestyle change that will benefit animals. This might be donating a few bucks to an animal shelter, getting a birdbath, going vegetarian one day per week, or anything else that you feel guided and willing to do.

8

Plant Allies

INDOORS AND OUTDOORS, plants are beings of magic. In addition to cleaning the air, healing any number of physical and emotional ills, and looking beautiful, they also move the energy around in a healthy way, summon fairies and nature spirits, and lend their unique magical personalities to the space and your life. Cultivating relationships with plants is also an effective way to get in touch with the subtler realms of information and communication, and can activate your natural intuitive abilities by opening your third eye, the energy center located just above your eyebrows.

In this chapter, I discuss some of my favorite plant allies and offer some ideas for how to work with them in and around your space. The list is in no way comprehensive, but it is my intention that the descriptions will inspire you to learn to recognize the magical properties of, and cultivate relationships with, all plants on a deep, energetic level.

Coming into intuitive alignment with the unique personalities and needs of plants will help you care for them effectively, even if you think you're "no good with plants." For example, instead of watering at fixed intervals, like exactly once a week or once a day, you might try relaxing your mind and silently asking the plant if he's ready for some water. If the answer is yes, see if you can stop watering when you intuitively hear the plant say when. Also, I find that plants don't like to be fussed over, and if you worry about them too much or care for them excessively, they tend to suffer.

That being said, you may (as I do) still run into some problems with your plants. Even though you feel like you're doing everything right, a houseplant or flower might mysteriously suffer. If this happens and you don't want to get rid of the plant yet, do your very best to resuscitate the plant for up to a month. If, after that time, you can't perceive that you've made any progress, and if you don't know someone who'd like to adopt the plant and attempt to revive it, return the plant to the earth by moving the plant to the compost heap or yard waste bin. I know this might sound harsh and cruel, and I won't lie, it breaks my heart to think of it. But it is, unfortunately, necessary, because having a chronically suffering plant is much worse than having no plant at all. For one thing, this is because the plant isn't happy and doesn't like living that way. But it's also a representation of struggle and suffering in the energetic body of your home, which of course mirrors your own body and personal life.

And, as my mom always says, you get along with some plants and not with others, just like people. This means you must, through both intuition and trial and error, learn which plants thrive under your care and which plants don't. The plants that thrive are your allies. For example, for me, jade is my ally, and miniature roses are not. I like and admire other people's miniature roses, but I know that something about my energy does not allow them to thrive while under my care.

You'll find that in my plant descriptions, I refer to the plants as he or she. This is because plants are living organisms with unique personalities, and so referring to a plant as an "it" just doesn't feel right to me.

As you read these, keep in mind that I'm describing my personal relationships and experiences with the plants, and that yours might be quite different. I recommend that you think of each description as a jumping-off point for your own relationship, as if I'm introducing you and the plant at a party.

Aloe

Aloe is like a botanical avatar, as she is a physical manifestation of pure, unconditional love. I don't usually recommend living with blade-shaped plants, as generally speaking they are not terribly friendly, but aloe is a notable exception. She's a master healer, able to speed the healing of both physical and emotional wounds. After you plant her, tune in to her energy and have a conversation with her, asking her to help you with any aspect of healing or heart opening. You can plant her anywhere, but the front left corner of your front yard (when facing the house from the sidewalk or street) will be especially helpful for general healing and increased heart opening, and the back right corner of your back yard will help with healing and love issues that have to do with romance, such as a broken heart or emotional trauma. Because her energy is so expansively loving and open, she keeps negativity away. Also, as you may already know, you can break off a piece of aloe and use the gel inside as an unsurpassed healing balm for burns and sometimes for cuts (though this does not substitute for an antibiotic). And if you or someone in your family could use a little extra support with healing, you can enlist the help of aloe with the aloe healing ritual below.

Aloe grows best outdoors or in a pot near a window, in full sun or part shade. Also, aloe doesn't like a lot of fuss, and hardly ever likes to be watered. She likes to give more than she likes to receive.

. . . .

Aloe Healing Ritual

This ritual will enlist an aloe plant to powerfully support your (or another member of your household's) healing process. It helps to heal both physical and emotional conditions.

INGREDIENTS:

    1 aloe plant, indoors in a pot or outdoors
      in a garden, planter, or pot

    1 piece of rose quartz (be sure to cleanse—see chapter 6)

Sit in front of the aloe plant and hold the rose quartz in your hands. Take some deep breaths and relax. Begin to tune in to the energy of the aloe plant. When you feel ready, mentally or aloud, have a conversation with the aloe plant. Tell her what you're healing from, and ask her to assist you in your healing process. Also charge the rose quartz with your intention to heal. Then bury the rose quartz near the base of the aloe plant as an offering. Thank the aloe for her help, and care for her lovingly and sparingly—remember: she loves sunlight but doesn't like a lot of attention.

Bamboo (Indoor)

Bamboo has a very happy and uplifting energy. First and foremost, he brings joy. Secondarily, the joy can express itself as increased success, luck, and wealth. This is because joy is magnetic and draws happy conditions. I like to put living bamboo in the bathroom to counterbalance the downward pull of energy, or in the health and family relationships, gratitude and prosperity, radiance and reputation, or serenity and self-love area to enhance the energies associated with the respective area. He's also a good plant to bring into any area that feels cold and sterile, as he brings feelings of aliveness and laughter. And he's a great friend to have if you're helping yourself to move out of a funk or depression.

Bamboo has such a happy and sunshiny energy in and of himself that he's not big on direct sunlight. He might live, but he'll likely lose his color or his leaves will dry out. Just keep him in fresh water and out of direct light. He can even thrive in a windowless room.

Basil

Basil is quite a dashing little fellow. He bestows everyone's favorite magical gifts: love, passion, wealth, luck, and attractiveness. Planting basil anywhere in your front yard will help you to be uncommonly beautiful and bewitching. If you'd like to give your luck and finances a boost, plant basil near the front door or anywhere along the back edge of the back yard. Cooking a meal with fresh basil, such as pasta al pesto, will enhance passion and love for you and whomever you feed it to. Putting basil leaves into a floor wash will invite prosperity and luck.

Living with basil in your garden brings a deep magic and other-worldliness to the energy of your home. And, as in the basil bath below, bathing with a few leaves of fresh basil can enhance your attractiveness.

Basil grows best outdoors in full sunlight.

. . . .

Bewitching Basil Bath

This bath is great for anytime you'd like to turn up the volume on your attractiveness until it reaches the "bewitching" level. The effects last around six hours and then start to slowly fade back to normal, so it's great for a specific event that you'd like to look your best for, like a date, a party, or an interview. Oh, and only do it once per moon cycle, or it'll stop working.

INGREDIENTS:

    6 fresh basil leaves

    ½ cup organic powdered sugar

    1 stick vanilla incense

    A white or off-white candle

Draw a warm to hot bath. Place the candle and incense near the bathtub and light. Put the basil and sugar in the water and stir it around a bit in a clockwise direction with your right hand. Hold your palms over the water and visualize very bright white light pouring down from above, through the crown of your head, down to your heart, through your arms, and out through your hands and into the water. Imagine the water swirling and pulsating with the magnetic energy of bewitching attractiveness. Soak in the bath for 40 minutes, or until the incense burns all the way down. Feel free to read during your bath, but only read things that are uplifting and positive.

Cyclamen

Cyclamen is a dear friend of mine and has helped me through some tough times. She's the psychotherapist of the garden, helping with deeply imbedded issues regarding sexuality and abuse. When you care for cyclamen, she cares for you by reaching gently into your energetic field and pulling out the issues so that you can deal with them and release them to the soul of the earth for composting and deep purification. Cyclamen is also just a good gal to have around to help you process your feelings. Choose a color or colors that feel healing and comforting to you.

Cyclamen grows best outdoors in full sun in milder climates and part shade in hotter ones.

Golden Pothos

Golden pothos is the prince of indoor plants. He cleans the air while filling in stagnant areas above high cupboards or shelves with his abundant, flowing leaves or cascading down from hanging planters like a fountain of green, golden-streaked, heart-shaped cash. He has a very friendly, uplifting, purifying, and abundant energy, and he's very easy to care for.

All golden pothos needs is love and a light, occasional watering. He usually does well in any type of indoor light.

Hydrangea

Hydrangea is the old wise woman of the garden. In the blink of an eye, she can see deeply into the hearts and minds of all humans, whether they enter your space physically or merely send their energy in the form of a spell, prayer, or intention.

Not only that, but she can immediately unravel, transmute, and redirect all negativity and ill will, so that you're safe from psychic attack, physical harm, and general bad vibes. She must be enlisted for this purpose, so when you plant her, mentally have a conversation with her, respectfully asking her to watch over and protect the energy that surrounds and enters your home. Her responsiveness to subtle changes in energy can be perceived by her habit of changing color as a result of slight changes in the pH of the soil. She's best in the front yard for protective purposes, but you can plant her in the back yard as well for an extra protective kick if you feel in some way vulnerable about your back entrances or windows, or just because she looks pretty. And if you like, you can formally employ hydrangea's security skills with the ritual below.

Hydrangea grows best outdoors in full sun. In very hot climates, she likes a bit of shade.

. . . .

Hydrangea Security System

Please note: this ritual is (of course) not a substitute for actually physically securing your home, as the ephemeral world of magic always works in tandem with the physical world of form so that the two worlds can support and regulate one another.

INGREDIENTS:

A number of hydrangea plants, any color

A stick of frankincense incense

1 piece of white quartz for each plant (make sure you cleanse them—see chapter 6)

The number of hydrangeas you'll want to obtain depends on your setup and enthusiasm. For example, for an apartment, you could just have one in a pot by the front door; for a house, you could plant tons of hydrangeas all around the perimeter, or just one, or two by the front door and one by the back door, etc. If you want to really pour on the protective vibes, you might want to get a bunch.

Before you plant and/or position the hydrangeas, assemble them in a central location and place the incense near them, but not so close that it will burn them or heat them up uncomfortably. Ideally, the smoke will move up and around their leaves, so you might try putting the incense near the center of them if you've got a few. Light the incense. Hold the quartz pieces in your hands and take some deep breaths. Now tune in to the hydrangeas and communicate with them, either mentally or aloud. Remember that they are very wise. They'll understand in a very deep way if you explain exactly why you're asking for their help and exactly the types of people and/or energy you'd like them to protect you from. Once you've told them your wishes, see if you can perceive them accepting the mission (which they will). Then, tell them thank you from the bottom of your heart and bury a quartz piece near each of their bases. Now you're ready to position them or plant them in strategic places near your home.

Jade

Jade is a succulent, with small, round, shiny green leaves. For me, there are some plants that feel like members of my immediate family, and jade is one of those plants. For many years, I've lived with at least one jade. Jade emanates a strong but subtle prosperity energy and helps you learn to feel sturdy and stable with regard to finances. Her traits demonstrate prosperous abilities. For example, she can multiply herself exponentially: if you put a small cutting of jade in water, she'll grow roots, and then you can plant her in a pot or outside. Then, she thrives and appears moist and vibrant with very little water. She does well in full sun or total shade. When you care for jade, she's like a kind and patient teacher who shares her prosperity secrets through example.

Jade grows best indoors or outdoors, in sun or shade. Her motto is "waste not, want not," and therefore she strongly dislikes being overwatered. Outside, she might not want to be watered at all, unless she's in a pot.

Lavender

Lavender is a longtime ally of magical folk. She has a sweet, soothing, relaxing, and rejuvenating fragrance and a very high spiritual vibration. She entices fairies to enter your garden in droves and to dwell there, which brings great blessings to all areas of life. Lavender in the front yard can purify and uplift people and energetic vibrations as they leave the outside world and enter the sacred and magical space that is your home.

Lavender grows best outdoors in full sunlight.

Norfolk Island Pine

Norfolk Island pine is a gem. He's a hearty yet gentle soul, and he happily absorbs excess negativity and transforms it into love. (This action is mirrored in the physical realm as he draws toxins out of the air.) He softens the effects of harsh words and feelings and helps create a general feeling of peace and harmony in the space. Keeping a potted Norfolk Island pine is also a great alternative to the unnecessary killing of baby trees at Christmas. You can dress him up for December, and then he can go back to being his normal, unadorned self the rest of the year.

Norfolk Island pine does best indoors, near a window.

Rose

The rose is the ascended master of the garden. Cultivated yet purely natural and wildly beautiful, she is said to have the highest vibration of all living things. Bringing her into your yard brings feelings of spiritual devotion, inspiration, and connection with All That Is. Her energy is also very romantic, passionate, and purifying. While roses appear in countless shades and variations of colors, here are some additional traits for various colors:

> **Fuchsia:** passion for life, self-love, love and acceptance of your physical body and appearance
>
> **Lavender:** enlightened spirituality and physical beauty
>
> **Peach:** peace, gentleness, spirituality, friendship
>
> **Pink:** especially romantic love, sweet, fun, playful
>
> **Red:** especially passionate; deep, true, physical and spiritual romantic love that cuts deep into the heart
>
> **White:** especially purifying and healing; connection with universal love / light energy
>
> **White with Red Speckles:** pure devotion speckled with deep and abiding passion

Yellow: I only recommend planting yellow roses
if you also plant red and pink roses nearby.
Yellow roses have a very grounding energy,
which is good, but without red and pink they
can bring feelings of boredom, jealousy, and/or
stuckness to the love and romance department.

Roses grow best outdoors in full sun, with perhaps a splash of shade.

Rose Geranium

Rose geranium is like the diva of the garden, exceptionally feminine yet strong and dynamic as well. She's all about the heart chakra. She opens your heart to love, brings sweetness, raises vibrations, and entices the fairies of romance to hang around.

Rose geranium grows best outdoors in full sun. If the climate is especially hot, she likes to sit in the shade during the hot hours of the afternoon.

Rosemary

An old friend of the wise ones, this herb is pungent and sweet at the same time. She lifts your spirits and energizes your conscious mind, enhancing clarity, positive mental focus, and magical power. Grown in the front yard, rosemary encourages the head female to publically "wear the pants" in the family. Grown in the back yard, rosemary lends behind-the-scenes strength and authority to the head female in the household, which is generally the more favorable of the two placements, as it usually lends itself more to harmony and balance for all. Still, either of these patterns can be positive or negative, depending on your relationship and situation. For example, if a relationship is out of balance, with the male wielding too much power and the female not enough, planting rosemary in the front yard can encourage a more balanced relationship. Wherever she is grown, rosemary transforms your garden into a powerful magical sanctuary. If you'd like advice about how to experience greater clarity and mental powers, rosemary is a great one to ask. Simply relax, tune in, and silently present your question. Then notice any impressions, images, or ideas that come into your mind. You might also like to place a bouquet of fresh rosemary in your workspace or study area for this purpose.

Rosemary grows best outdoors in full sunlight.

Rue

Rue doesn't mess around. She's a protective plant of great power, and she mightily neutralizes and repels negative spirits, vibrations, and entities. Because of rue's intensity, I don't recommend bringing her into your garden unless you're in serious need and feel besieged by negativity in any form. If you feel drawn to work with rue, plant her around the outside of your home, and ask her to deal with the negativity (in the form of spirits, people, situations, etc.) for you. If the plants happen to die, it could be that they absorbed and repelled so much negativity that it killed them. If this happens, thank them for their service and lovingly return them to the earth. Then smudge the inside and outside of your house with white sage, making sure to perform the three secrets empowerment to dissipate and repel any remaining negativity. Be careful with rue, because she causes skin irritation in some people.

Rue grows best outdoors in full sunlight.

Sage

If hydrangea is the wise woman, sage is the wise old man of the garden. The proverbial bearded guru at the top of a mountain, he has a very ancient and all-knowing energy (hence the name). Sage in the yard is both grounding and mystical. He purifies the energy with a deep earthy and airy scent and vibration while also subtly downloading his wisdom to you as you care for him. An additional benefit of growing sage is that you can pick lengths of stem containing leaves and dry them in a bundle tied with string to use as a smudge stick (see chapter 10).

Sage grows best outdoors in full sun.

9

Animal Allies

ANIMAL ALLIES IN and around our homes, living or artistically represented, generously bestow their unique magical energies and gifts upon us. Here are some animals that you may find helpful in your magical housekeeping practice, and some ideas for how to invite and encourage their presence in your home and life.

Bird (General)

Birds represent freedom, lightness, joy, divine messages, dreams taking flight, and the air element, which is about thoughts, words, and ideas. Because of these qualities, bird imagery is great for the radiance and reputation, creativity and playfulness, and serenity and self-love areas. They can be positive also for the synchronicity and miracles area because they represent swift travel and help from above. Make sure they never appear to be flying out the door or window, or away from the inside of the house or room, because this will symbolize a loss of energy and resources.

I don't generally recommend having birds as pets, as this requires a cage and sometimes involves the clipping of wings, neither of which is a positive affirmation for your own life, not to mention that they are far from pleasant for the bird. However, bird feeders, birdhouses, and birdbaths are all great ways to experience the magic of live birds around your home.

Butterfly

Butterflies represent transformation, rebirth, elevation from the mundane to the miraculous, beauty, romance, magic, imagination, and bliss. If you see a butterfly in your yard, it means fairies are present. Butterfly imagery is great for the radiance and reputation area, as a butterfly has transformed from a behind-the-scenes caterpillar into a spectacular winged creature, the indisputable superstar of the insect kingdom. An artistic representation of two butterflies in the love and marriage area can symbolize marital bliss. A picture or figure of one butterfly in the serenity and self-love area can support your efforts to transform your body, mind, and/or spirit. Butterfly imagery in the health and family relationships area can represent one or more loved ones who have passed from this life into the next. Butterflies in the creativity and playfulness area enhance inspiration and joy.

As tempting as it may be, please never, ever put cocoons in jars, as it's highly important to butterflies to sense the open air around them as they metamorphose.

Cat

My favorite. Cats are sacred and represent magical power, intuition, and wisdom. They also represent independence, sensuality, freedom, cleanliness, calm ferocity, agility, and secrecy. Cats are in alignment with nighttime, feminine lunar energy.

It can be helpful to bring one or more artistic representations of cats into your serenity and self-love area, radiance and reputation area, or creativity and playfulness area to enhance any of these life areas with the magical energies associated with cats.

Cats are my dear allies and family members, so forgive me if I seem overbearing, but I must share a bit of advice for anyone living with, or considering living with, a cat or cats:

- Don't declaw! It's not like removing fingernails, it's like removing *fingers*. Cats use their claws for everything. If you're concerned about your furniture, and even if you aren't, get a scratching post.

- If you have one cat, consider getting two so they can keep each other company when you're gone. (Especially if your cat stays inside all the time.) And if you bring in a second cat that's a bit younger in age than the first and is the opposite sex, they might make friends a bit more quickly. Having two cats is also a positive affirmation of a healthy relationship, and it helps the unique aspects of your cats' personalities to become known to you as you notice the differences between them.

- I don't even have to say spay and neuter, of course, because you already know.

- Give them organic and/or fresh catnip. It's their dearest ally in the plant kingdom, and who are we to deny them of it? (But if they are still less than a year old, they might not be too into it yet.)

- Rescue! Please don't financially support breeders when there are so many homeless cats in the world.

Of course you shouldn't adopt a cat for this reason alone, but having a cat in your home moves the energy around in a healthy way, as cats tend to climb, explore, and get into every nook and cranny, which stirs and circulates the energy and keeps it fresh.

Dog

Oh, how I love dogs. Did I say cats were my favorite? Well, so are dogs. They represent loyalty, friendship, playfulness, happiness, protection, and unconditional love, and they bring these qualities into your life.

Images of dogs in the radiance and reputation area or creativity and playfulness area will lend their magical properties to these areas of your life.

If you live with or are thinking of living with a dog or dogs, here are my two cents about treating them with love and respect:

- Let the dog in the house, and let the dog sleep in the house. It's not spiritually or magically rewarding to have a superiority complex about your species. Plus, it gets very cold and very hot outside.

- Seriously consider letting the dog on the bed and sofa. If the state of your décor is more important than the comfort and happiness of your best friend, your priorities may need revisiting.

- Also don't adopt a dog unless you can give the dog a lot of time and attention. These guys live for love and companionship, 24/7. Think of adopting a dog almost the same way you would think of adopting a human.

- Again, I know I don't even have to tell you, but spay and neuter.

- Rescue! Please don't financially support breeders when there are so many homeless dogs in the world. Plus, paying for a designer dog is so last century. (If you really must have a certain breed, try looking for rescue organizations for specific breeds, such as "poodle rescue.")

Dragon

Dragons represent expansiveness, raging success, fame, good luck, and good fortune. To bring these qualities into your life, the radiance and reputation area is the best place for dragon imagery. But be ready: the results can be intense, especially when coupled with the three secrets empowerment. Speaking of intense results, check out the charm below.

. . . .

Famous Dragon Charm

This is a charm that will help you to express and expand your personal power and be recognized for your wonderful talents. (Not everyone wants to be on the cover of *People*, but there are other ways to be famous, like being famous in certain circles or famous for certain unique talents or abilities.)

INGREDIENTS:

> A dragon patch that you like (idea:
>   check karate supply websites)
> Red, bright orange, or hot pink felt
> Red, orange, yellow, pink, and/or gold ribbon
> A tassel that matches the ribbon
> Dried calendula (an herb) and/or dried sunflower petals
> Needle and thread

Cut two squares of felt just big enough for the patch to fit comfortably on one. Turn one of the squares 45 degrees so that it's a diamond, and sew the patch on it. Sew the squares together around the edges, leaving one side open. Stuff the charm with the calendula and/or sunflower petals and sew closed. Attach the ribbon or ribbons in a loop from the top corner of the diamond, and attach the tassel from the bottom corner so that it hangs down. Hold it in both hands, take some deep breaths, close your eyes, and visualize/feel/sense yourself radiating your unique light out into the world in a joyful way. Also visualize/feel/sense what it will be like to be known and recognized in the world in all the ways you most want to be known and recognized. You might imagine your phone ringing off the hook, or crowds cheering, or receiving an award, or whatever will happen when the world takes notice of your talents in a big way. In other words, let yourself daydream extravagantly and feel good about it. Then mentally direct very bright golden light (like sunlight) into the charm. Hang the charm somewhere in your radiance and reputation area, and get ready for your close-up.

Dragonfly

Dragonflies are filled with fairy energy. If you see a dragonfly in your yard, you can be sure the fairies are close by. Dragonflies are otherworldly creatures; as a bridge between our everyday realm and the realm of the fairies, they help guide us toward the border of these worlds so that we may begin to see beyond the thin veil between them.

Dragonfly imagery in the radiance and reputation area will enhance the way you are known in the world, and dragonfly imagery in the creativity and playfulness area will deepen your sense of whimsy and magic and enhance your imaginative endeavors.

Fish

Fish represent joyful equanimity and abundance. Because of this, fish imagery is great for the gratitude and prosperity area and serenity and self-love area. Also, if the fish imagery is whimsical, it can be great for the creativity and playfulness area. Fish imagery can be challenging, however, if the fish appear to be swimming out the door or toward the outside of the house. This will symbolize energy flowing away from you rather than toward you.

Some of you, including many feng shui consultants, will not agree with me on this, but I don't recommend inviting live fish to live in your house or yard (although ponds are generally better than aquariums). This is because, unlike cats and dogs, adoptable fish are all either bred or captured, which is not cool with me because I don't like to treat animals any way that I wouldn't want to be treated. And because they aren't naturally domesticated, any aquarium or pond will be a form of imprisonment to them, and imprisoned animals in and around our homes would indicate and perpetuate feelings of imprisonment in certain areas of our own lives. Also, in aquariums and ponds, fish are completely dependent on our ability to keep their water at the perfect temperature, cleanliness, and alkalinity, and to feed them exactly the right amount of food, which in my opinion is a lot of pressure. That being said, some of you might be the best fish caretakers ever, and you might be so tuned in to your fish that you can tell by looking at them that they're happy as clams (no lame joke intended). If that's the case, far be it from me to intervene.

As an alternative to actual fish, I have a computer-animated DVD of an aquarium that looks very real, and I love to invite fish energy into my home by transforming my television into a virtual aquarium.

Frog

Frogs represent the water element and bring luck and good fortune. A frog statue by the door calls in good fortune, and frog imagery is also good in the gratitude and prosperity area for this purpose. Frogs are not fond of captivity, and I don't recommend keeping them as pets.

Hidden Frog Good Luck Greeter

This is a simple yet super-powerful ritual that will bring a generous supply of good luck, sweetness, and good fortune into your life.

INGREDIENTS:

A potted jade plant

A tiny plastic, rubber, or ceramic frog

15 bright, shiny pennies

On the day or evening of the new moon, place the jade plant near your front door. Hold the frog in your cupped hands. Bring it up near your mouth and whisper:

> *Thank you for bringing me*
> *good luck and good fortune.*

Place the frog in the jade plant so that he's turned toward any visitors that might appear at your doorstep, as if he's spying on them. (He doesn't need to be completely hidden, but it's best if he's not terribly noticeable, which shouldn't be too difficult, since he's so tiny.) Then bury one penny somewhere around the base of the jade as an offering to the jade and the frog. Every day or evening, lean down to the frog, cup your hands around your mouth, and whisper again:

> *Thank you for bringing me*
> *good luck and good fortune.*

Then, bury another one of the pennies. Continue this practice once per day until they're all buried, which will be on the day of the full moon.

Horse

Horses represent wildness, rebelliousness, strength, and freedom. If you choose horse art, I suggest imagery that depicts them in their wild, rather than domesticated, state. Also, make sure they don't appear to be running out the door or away from the house, as this would represent and perpetuate a loss of energy and resources.

Imagery of two horses in the love and marriage area can be a positive affirmation of a relationship in which both partners retain their personal power and freedom. Horses enhance the way you're seen in the world when placed in the radiance and reputation area. In the creativity and playfulness area, they help you to express your wild creativity. And in the serenity and self-love area, they can help you get back in touch with your strength, wildness, and freedom.

Hummingbird

Hummingbirds are pure joy, energy, sweetness, very high vibrations, happy manifestation of your deep desires, the light and fun aspects of romantic love, and fairy energy.

I have a hummingbird feeder just outside the radiance and reputation area of my house, and since it's been up my songwriting boyfriend and I have been having a magical amount of radiance and reputation-style success in our respective careers. Not only that, but we have hummingbirds visiting all the time, and it always brightens our day to greet them.

If you hang a hummingbird feeder, make sure to keep the nectar fresh by rinsing the feeder and replacing the nectar every week or so. You can hang one anywhere in your yard, but other especially good places for hummingbird feeders would be near the outside of your love and marriage area to bring energy and sweetness to your love life, or near the outside of your creativity and playfulness area to bring energy and imagination to your artistic projects and a sense of fun and magic to your life. If there's an area of your yard where no one ever goes, like a side yard that's fenced off, it's a good idea to put some kind of bird feeder (hummingbird or other) in this area just to bring in some vibrant energy and movement. No matter where you hang it, it's best if you can see the feeder through a window from the inside of your house so that you can enjoy it and also so you'll remember to keep the nectar fresh.

Lion

Lions teach us how to be the king or queen of our destiny. If you're ready to shine your light with a regal and authoritative air, you might want to work with lion imagery in your space. Lions also represent calm ferocity, the sun, and the fire element.

In the radiance and reputation area, lions help us to be known as powerful and royal, and help us to assert our authority in the outside world. In the serenity and self-love area, lions help us to respect our own power and to assert our authority in our own lives.

Owl

Owls represent divine feminine energy, lunar and nighttime energy, wisdom, secrets, and the afterlife. If you'd like to be well known and well respected in your field while staying behind the scenes, owl imagery would be good in your radiance and reputation area. If you'd like to enhance your wisdom, alignment with the moon, and/or occult knowledge, owl imagery in your serenity and self-love area would be appropriate.

Snake

In Judeo-Christian circles, snakes get a very bad rap. This could be because snakes represent very ancient feminine power as well as sensuality and connection with the earth. Oh, I know all about the Eden story. It just seems rather too convenient that the snake was so effectively vilified in the story of Eve's fall from grace. I'm probably just paranoid.

At any rate, let's review: the snake represents very ancient feminine power, sensuality, and connection with the earth. Snake imagery would be great in the radiance and reputation area if you'd like to be known as a very powerful female. Snakes would also be good in the serenity and self-love area if you're working on reclaiming the fullness of your feminine power or if you'd like to align yourself more deeply with Goddess and earth energy.

Sorry, but no pet snakes. Snakes want to be free!

Spider

Spiders represent creativity, fate, magical ability, and divine feminine energy. If you're like most people, you may not feel particularly inclined to live with spiders or spider imagery. However, because they are not only living beings but also longtime allies of magical folk, I feel it's particularly important to refrain from killing them or destroying their webs unnecessarily. If you find a spider in your house, consider trapping it under a cup, sliding a thin piece of cardboard under the cup, and releasing the spider outside. (Incidentally, I just did this successfully with a mosquito, which I was quite proud of.) In addition to saving a life, another benefit of the cup/cardboard spider removal method is that you get to ask the spider a question, as you'll learn more about in the "Ask the Spider" section below.

You'll probably feel it necessary (as I do) to destroy spider webs you find inside the house, but outside the house I suggest that you merely step around them, unless they are directly in the middle of a much-used pathway or somewhere they're likely to be accidentally destroyed anyway (which could be traumatic for the accidental destroyer). I find that spiders share ancient magical wisdom and inspiration with you when you consciously admire their handiwork, and for this reason (and for purely aesthetic reasons) I've cultivated an appreciation for the fine art of web spinning. If you have an irrational fear of spiders, it might be a good idea to investigate this fear through meditation, journaling, and/or visualization. It's very likely that moving beyond this fear will allow your magical abilities to be more available to you.

If you do feel inclined to live with spider imagery, a spider or spiders in the creativity and playfulness area would fuel your imagination and creative projects. The radiance and reputation area would only be a good place for spider imagery if you're like I was when I was when I was in high school and you'd like to be known in an offbeat and goth sort of way, like Marilyn Manson or Elvira. This is because spiders aren't particularly highly regarded in mainstream society. The serenity and self-love area is a good place for spider imagery if you are studying magic or the intuitive arts.

I don't recommend keeping tarantulas or any other spiders as pets, as this would cause them to be imprisoned almost certainly against their will.

. . . .

Ask the Spider

As I mentioned, whenever you rescue a spider instead of killing it, you get the privilege of asking her one question and receiving an answer. The best kinds of questions to ask spiders have to do with creativity, magical ability, and/or intuition. For example, you might ask the spider something like "What should my next creative project be?" or "How can I increase my intuitive abilities?" As you take the spider from inside the house to outside the house, mentally explain to her that you're putting her outside as a favor, so that you don't have to kill her. She'll understand, because she knows what killing an accidental guest is all about. Then ask your question, mentally or aloud, just as you're releasing the spider outside. After you ask your question, be alert but patient. Your answer will present itself, usually in a very quiet yet unmistakable way, sometime within the following six days.

Turtle/Tortoise

Turtles and tortoises represent the earth element, stability, and longevity, and their imagery is very grounding and comforting. If you're feeling stressed out or unsafe, or like your energy is all over the place, it might be a good idea to bring in a statue or picture of a turtle to mellow you out and bring you down to earth. Good places to place turtle imagery for this purpose would be the synergy, balance, and bliss area and the serenity and self-love area.

Turtles and tortoises are not naturally domesticated and prefer living in the wild, so I don't recommend adopting them.

. . . .

Turtle Statue Empowerment Ritual
(for Slowness, Steadiness, and Winning the Race)

If you feel like you're not able to enjoy life because you always seem to be rushing around all over the place, trying to accomplish a seemingly insurmountable number of things, this ritual will be just the thing.

Obtain a stone or ceramic turtle or tortoise statue that you really like. (It can be any size—just choose something appropriate to the area in which you decide to place it.) You can place it near your workspace, near your front door, near your meditation area, or in your serenity / self-love area—whichever feels most powerful to you.

Place your hands on the statue and tune in to the tortoise's cool earthiness and solidity. Close your eyes and visualize/ imagine/feel yourself as very grounded, serene, and relaxed; also see yourself easily and effortlessly finishing everything on your to-do list and accomplishing everything you wish to accomplish. Feel the feelings that will go along with this eventuality: relaxation, joy, enjoyment of life, pride in your accomplishments, etc. Then say:

> *I am grounded. I am serene. I easily accomplish*
> *everything on my to-do list. I am mindful of the*
> *beauty of the present moment. I always have plenty*
> *of time. All of my endeavors result in success. Thank*
> *you, thank you, thank you. Blessed be. And so it is.*

10

Sacred Smoke & Aromas of Power

NOTHING ENTICES, ENLIVENS, and elevates like scent. Smokes and aromas can relax, energize, heal, bless, uplift your mood, open the doors to the magical realms, stimulate creativity, increase abundance, enhance and increase romance, clear negativity from the space, call in good spirits, and more.

Magical Methods of Diffusion

Natural aromas can be diffused in a number of ways, each of which lends its unique magical slant. These include:

> Incense: Whether you prefer sticks, cones, or charcoal, burning incense is a very spiritual method of diffusing scent. With its smoke moving heavenward and into the ether, it's a gift to the Divine. It can help carry wishes, intentions, and prayers into the realm of infinite creativity, where they are planted as seeds that eventually manifest into form. Incense can also

elevate an everyday room into a more mystical plane of existence.

Smudging: Smudging is the burning of dried, bundled herbs and is most commonly done with white sage, desert sage, and sweetgrass. Smudge sticks are held in the hand while smoke rises from them, and the smoke is directed around a space to transform or enhance the energy in a specific way, depending on the plant and intention.

Oils: All-natural essential oils can be diffused in an oil burner, plug-in diffuser, or other commercial aromatherapy-diffusing product. You can also pour boiling water into a mug, bowl, or pot with a few drops of oil to release the scent with the steam. Essential oils work on an emotional level. Various scents and blends support and transform us in different ways, and they can help heal old patterns, lend fresh ideas and perspectives, and positively affect health and mood in a number of ways.

Aromatherapy Mists: Diffusible potions made with essential oils, flower and gem essences, pure water, and the power of intention, aromatherapy mists work on emotional and vibrational levels and allow you to finely attune and calibrate the energy of your space.

Candles: Soy or vegetable wax candles made with essential oils also infuse a room with natural scent.* In addition to the positive benefits of diffusing natural essential oils, burning candles calls good spirits and divine energy and aliveness to your space. Candles, like incense, can also assist with manifestation when you light them with specific intentions in mind.

Below, you'll discover the magical and metaphysical properties and uses of various types of incense, smudge sticks, and oils, and you'll also learn how to create your own magical aromatherapy mists and burn candles in your space to help set a mood or manifest an intention.

Incense

Cedar

Cedar draws upon both earthly energies and divine energies simultaneously, and it is therefore highly spiritual in nature. It cleanses energy and protects from unwanted negative energy and influences by lifting vibrations and calling in divine masculine energy. Cedar can strengthen health, clarity, and resolve, and it encourages meditation, prayer, and other spiritual pursuits.

Cinnamon

Cinnamon has a very high and happy vibration. It brings warmth and joy and gets energy moving in a healthy way. It's also very spiritual and accesses high levels of awareness to teach us about the spiritual aspects of living an abundant life, includ-

---

* I *do* recommend having a junk drawer, because there are some things that just don't seem to go anywhere else. Just make sure you clear it often.

ing loving ourselves deeply, treating ourselves well, lightening up, following our unique paths, releasing our outmoded money concepts and beliefs, and being willing to receive.

Copal

Copal opens the doors between realms and calls good spirits into your space. It can also be used for very deep cleansing and releasing of sticky negative energy, as would be necessary in the case of an earthbound entity (a.k.a. an unhappy ghost) living in the home. (See the next chapter for more about ghosts.)

Frankincense

Frankincense is pure spirituality. It lifts vibrations, protects, cleanses, creates sacred space, and aligns you with the Divine.

Nag Champa

For me, there's just something about Nag Champa (pronounced *nahg CHAHmpah* and affectionately referred to as "the nahgs") that transports me to another world in the sweetest and most delicious of ways. To many incense lovers, Nag Champa is the old standby because of its reasonable price and consistent ability to elevate consciousness and ambience. It smells sweet, vaguely floral, earthy, and airy all at once. I think of it as the magical all-purpose incense. It calls blessings, divine energy, and sweet spirits, helps with manifesting anything you like (romance, abundance, success, creativity, etc.), cleanses negativity, lifts vibrations, relaxes the mind, soothes the body, and uplifts the spirit. One of the many who share my love of Nag Champa is Bob Dylan, who likes to burn it in large quantities at his concerts.

Patchouli

Patchouli is pure Earth Goddess energy, and as such, it allows us to luxuriate in physical pleasures by connecting us with our bodies and the abundant blessings of the physical realm. Patchouli connects us with the earth, helps us manifest abundance, and helps us enjoy the physical aspects of harmonious romance. If you've felt "in your head" or "all over the place," patchouli incense might be just the thing to bring you back into your body and into a glorious enjoyment of the present moment and all the blessings it brings.

Rose

Rose incense brings the energy of the Goddess in her Divine Mother form, and it is therefore sweet, nurturing, receptive, loving, and open. Rose vibrates at a very high level, so it is also quite spiritual and uplifting. In incense form, it helps manifest the spiritual aspects of harmonious romance.

Vanilla

Vanilla incense is sweet, airy, and earthy, and calls in blessings of romance, luxury, and abundance. Vanilla incense helps with manifesting by helping you love yourself exactly as you are, which of course frees up the channels to receiving what you desire.

Smudge Sticks

Smudge sticks are tied-up or braided bundles of dried herbs that are carried and burned like incense around a room or area in order to create energetic shifts with the magical power of the smoke.

You can purchase smudge sticks online or at many health and metaphysical stores, or you can make your own. To make your own sage smudge stick, simply cut fresh sage and tie it firmly into a wandlike bundle with hemp twine or cotton string. Then hang it to dry. For sweetgrass braids, you're on your own—I've never made one myself, but I imagine it's pretty easy if you know where and how to find fresh sweetgrass (which I don't).

White Sage Bundles

If you only have one magical housekeeping tool or ingredient, a white sage bundle should be it. This is because burning white sage lifts vibrations, releases stuck energy, protects from negativity, and creates sacred space. If any sort of negative event takes place in your space, you can burn white sage to quickly and effectively purify the residual energy from the event. It is also just a good practice to burn it periodically for general purification. After you burn it, you'll definitely notice a positive difference in the feeling and atmosphere of a room.

To burn it, just light the bundle and carefully shake it over a dish or the sink until the flame goes out but it is still smoking. Carry a dish under the burning tip to catch any falling ash, and move around the perimeter of each room you'd like to purify, taking as much time with each area as your intuition guides you to. You can also burn it around your body to purify your energetic body and aura.

Desert Sage Bundles

Desert sage also clears energy but in a different way. While white sage purifies by lifting vibrations and dissolving negativity, desert sage moves the vibrations around in a happy way so that bad vibes just naturally don't feel like hanging out. For this reason, it has been used as a magical "road-opener." If you've been feeling stuck in your life, and you'd like to clear the way for new opportunities and unexpected avenues, burning desert sage in your home and around your aura is a good idea. Concentrate especially at thresholds and doors, in order to open new doors in your life. Its smoke has a very sweet personality and can create feelings of safety, coziness, and playfulness. Desert sage is good to burn in a new place to help you feel relaxed and at ease in the new environment, and to help make it your own. It can also call spirits of ancestors and deceased loved ones into your space.

Sweetgrass Braids

Sweetgrass smells delicious, and when you burn it, you can immediately sense its sweet and earthy-yet-otherworldly personality. Rather than removing negative vibes, sweetgrass summons positive ones in the form of beneficent deceased loved ones, angels, guides, animal guides, gods/goddesses, and ascended masters, all of whom are great to have around for a number of reasons, including protection, happiness, and receiving messages from beyond. You might like to cleanse the space with sage before you invite in helpers with sweetgrass. Then, as you light it and as you burn it, mentally or aloud invite sweet and helpful spirits to enter your home. (See ritual on page 107.)

Oils

I like to diffuse essential oils in my oil burner, which is like a potpourri burner only with a smaller dish on top. You just put water in the top dish, light a tealight below, and put a few drops of your chosen oil or blend of oils in the water. You can also purchase other types of essential oil diffusers or create a simple makeshift diffuser by pouring boiling water in a ceramic cup or bowl and putting a few drops of oil in the water. This will continue to diffuse the scent for only as long as the steam is rising, but it can still do a pretty good job of scenting a room.

> **Angelica:** dissolves and evacuates negative vibes and entities; helps to remove any type of heavy, dark, or sticky energy from the space

> **Cedar:** strengthening and purifying; creates sacred space with high spiritual vibrations

> **Cinnamon:** lifts and circulates energy in a healthy way; warming, uplifting, grounding, wealth-enhancing

> **Clary Sage:** creates clarity; purifies the space; profoundly uplifting, energizing, and encouraging

> **Clove:** warming, enhances psychic and magical powers, energizing, prosperity-drawing

> **Eucalyptus:** fresh, cooling, healing, purifying, energizing, exhilarating

> **Fennel:** cool, loving, receptive, healing, soothing, energizing

Jasmine: sensual, sweet, romantic, joyful, uplifting, enhances self-love and self-acceptance, soothes and opens the heart, encourages luxury, increases wealth (this oil is very expensive, and you might want to purchase it blended with a carrier oil or in absolute form)

Lavender: relaxing, soothing, calming, healing, stress-relieving

Lemon: energizing, uplifting, joyful, cleansing, purifying, raises vibrations, clears negativity

Neroli (Orange Blossom): joyful, relaxing, romantic, heart-opening; draws, strengthens, and harmonizes long-term relationships by encouraging self-love and self-acceptance

Patchouli: sensual, romantic, earthy; draws luxury and wealth

Peppermint: raises vibrations and creates clarity and calm; also cooling, energizing, uplifting, purifying

Rose: raises vibrations to a very high level of pure sweetness and love; purifying, harmonizing, heart-opening; calls angels and other highly vibrating beings of love (this oil is very expensive, and you might want to purchase it blended with a carrier oil or get rose absolute; alternatively, rose water has the same properties as rose oil and works great in a mister or oil burner)

Rose Geranium: lifts vibrations, opens the heart, strengthens the mind and body, lends courage, protects from negativity

Rosemary: creates clarity and amplifies memory and other mental abilities; energizing, uplifting, encouraging

Spearmint: soothing, comforting, gently purifying, cooling, uplifting

Tangerine: energizing, uplifting, joyful, cleansing, purifying; creates feelings of happiness and sweetness, moves the energy in a healthy way, calls in abundance

Vanilla: sweet, grounding, comforting, soothing, romantic

Ylang Ylang: heals issues with body image and sexuality; sensual, peaceful, relaxing, harmonizing, heart-opening

Aromatherapy Mists

Use these mists as you would a commercial room-freshening spray, and mist them generously throughout the room or house in order to infuse the space with their unique, custom-tailored magical vibrations. Spray them high into the air.

The gemstone and flower essences, as I described in the cleaning and gemstones chapters, are the vibration of the crystal or blossom preserved in water and alcohol. They're available online and at many metaphysical and health food stores.

· ·

Romance Mist

INGREDIENTS:

> Garnet essence or an actual garnet crystal
>
> Essential oil of jasmine or jasmine absolute
>
> Rose water in a mister

Put the garnet or 5 drops of garnet essence in the rose water. Then put 5–20 drops of jasmine in the rose water, depending on the strength of the oil and your personal preference. Shake well. Empower the bottle with the three secrets, being very specific with your intention and visualization.

· ·

Aura of Joy

INGREDIENTS:

> Hornbeam essence (a flower essence), apophyllite
>   essence (a gem essence), or an actual apophyllite
>
> Essential oil of neroli
>
> Essential oil of tangerine
>
> Essential oil of lemon
>
> Rose water in a mister

Put the apophyllite, 3 drops of apophyllite essence, or 3 drops of hornbeam essence in the rose water. Then put 10 drops of neroli, 5 of tangerine, and 3 of lemon in the mister. Shake. Hold the mister in both hands and visualize very bright, sparkly golden-white light filling the bottle. Feel the energy of laughter, smiles, vibrant energy, and high spirits entering and surrounding the liquid through the golden-white light. Also, if you like, feel free to further empower the liquid by saying a prayer and/or employing the three secrets.

Happy Home Mist

INGREDIENTS:

Citrine essence or an actual citrine

Essential oil of vanilla

Essential oil of tangerine

Essential oil of neroli

Spring water in a mister

During the daytime, when the sun is shining and not obscured by clouds, put the citrine or 5 drops of citrine essence in the mister, as well as 8 drops of vanilla, 3 drops of tangerine, and 6 drops of neroli. Shake. Visualize the pure, blinding, bright light of the sun coming down and entering the bottle, filling it completely. Ask for and feel very harmonious and happy vibrations entering the bottle along with the sunlight. Finish with the three secrets empowerment.

Peace and Harmony Mist

INGREDIENTS:

White chestnut essence

Amethyst essence or an actual amethyst

Essential oil of ylang ylang

Essential oil of lavender

Rose water in a mister

Put 4 drops of white chestnut essence and either 3 drops of amethyst essence or the amethyst into the mister. Then put 6 drops of ylang ylang and 8 drops of lavender in the mister. Shake. Hold the bottle in both hands, and visualize sparkly blue light entering the bottle along with vibrations of deep peace and profound harmony. Empower it with the three secrets, using the heart-calming mudra and the six true words.

. . . .

Angel Invitation Spray

This mist raises vibrations and opens the portals to the angelic realm to invite and receive angelic guests into your space.

INGREDIENTS:

> Aqua aura essence or an actual aqua aura
>
> Essential oil of rose or rose absolute
>
> Essential oil of neroli
>
> Rose water in a mister

Put the aqua aura or 4 drops of aqua aura essence in the mister. Then put up to 10 drops of the rose oil (depending on strength) and 6 drops of neroli in the mister. Shake. Hold the bottle in both hands, and visualize clear, sparkly light with shimmery rainbows in it spiraling down from the sky and filling the mister. Each time you spray, silently or aloud invite angels to enter your space. It's okay to invite them just because you'd like to have them around, but if you're inviting them for help with a specific purpose, tell them what you'd like help with and respectfully ask for their assistance in the matter.

. . . .

Fairy Invitation Spray

Sprinkle your home with fairy-friendly vibes, and welcome the magic. This mist is also very powerful for calling in ideal romantic conditions and enhancing self-love.

INGREDIENTS:

Lepidolite essence or an actual lepidolite

Essential oil of spearmint

Essential oil of vanilla

Essential oil of lavender

Rose water in a mister

Put the lepidolite or 5 drops of lepidolite essence in the mister. Add 4 drops of spearmint, 4 drops of vanilla, and 4 drops of lavender. Shake. Hold it in both hands, close your eyes, and visualize very bright, sparkly lavender light filling and surrounding the bottle.

. . . .

Goddess Invocation Mist

This mist calls in Goddess energy and helps invite the presence of the Goddess (in one or many of her forms) into your space and life. It's good for stress relief, hormonal balance, and balancing excess masculine energies (e.g., those present in a bachelor pad) with feminine energy. Using this mist is also an effective method of calling in a harmonious romance with a woman. For this or other specific purposes, make sure to couple it with the three secrets empowerment.

INGREDIENTS:

Moonstone essence or an actual moonstone

Essential oil of ylang ylang

Rose water in a mister

Put the moonstone or 5 drops of moonstone essence in the rose water. Put 7–10 drops of ylang ylang oil in the rose water. Shake. Hold the mist in both hands, and ask the Goddess to infuse it with her divine feminine energy. Visualize the bottle filled with the silvery, incandescent light of the moon.

. . . .

God Invocation Mist

This mist calls in divine masculine energy and invites the presence of the God (in one or many of his forms) into your space and life. It's good for increasing courage, confidence, and warrior energy, for lifting the vibrations to a sacred and spiritual level, and for balancing excess feminine energies (e.g., those present in a bachelorette pad) with masculine energy. This mist can also help you to call in a harmonious romance with a man. For this or other specific purposes, couple its use with the three secrets empowerment.

INGREDIENTS:

    Sunflower essence

    Essential oil of cedar

    Essential oil of frankincense

    Spring water in a mister

Put 4 drops of sunflower, 5 drops of cedar, and 5 drops of frankincense in the mister. Shake. Hold the bottle in both hands, and ask the God (in whatever form you choose) to infuse it with his divine masculine energy. Visualize it being filled with very bright, pure white light.

. . . .

Aura of Prosperity

Who couldn't use a little prosperity picker-upper?

INGREDIENTS:

    Citrine quartz essence or an actual citrine

    Essential oil of cinnamon

    Essential oil of tangerine

    Essential oil of patchouli (if you don't
      like patchouli, substitute neroli)

    Spring water in a mister

Put 9 drops of citrine essence or the actual citrine in the mister. Put 3 drops of each oil in the mister. Shake. Hold the bottle in both hands, and visualize very bright, sparkly emerald green light filling and surrounding it. For a specific intention, you might want to empower the mist with the three secrets.

· ·

Lighten Up Sparkle Spray

This one is a good one to have on hand for after an argument or for anytime things get too serious, heavy, or overwhelming. It's also a great support in times of grief or trauma. It creates perspective, loosens stuck energy, lifts the spirits, and enhances harmony and joy.

INGREDIENTS:

Lepidolite essence or an actual lepidolite

Apophyllite essence or an actual apophyllite

Bach Rescue Remedy

Essential oil of lavender

Essential oil of peppermint

Essential oil of spearmint

Rose water in a mister

Put 3 drops of lepidolite essence or the lepidolite, 3 drops of apophyllite essence or the apophyllite, and 4 drops of Rescue Remedy in the mister. Put 4 drops of lavender, 3 drops of peppermint, and 4 drops of spearmint in the mister. Shake. Hold the bottle in both hands, and visualize very bright, sparkly, robin's-egg blue light filling and surrounding the bottle.

Magic Stress Eraser Mist

Simple. It erases stress magically. If stress is a challenge for you, it might be a good idea to keep a travel mister of this in your purse or at your desk.

INGREDIENTS:

> Bach Rescue Remedy
>
> Essential oil of lavender
>
> Essential oil of peppermint
>
> Rose water in a mister

Put 4 drops of Rescue Remedy, 6 drops of lavender, and 4 drops of peppermint in the mister. Shake. Hold the bottle in both hands, and empower it with your intention to erase stress and create a peaceful, uplifting, and serene atmosphere. Visualize very bright white light filling the bottle.

Minty Mist for Physical Healing

This mist helps create an atmosphere that nurtures, supports, and encourages physical healing.

INGREDIENTS:

> Gardenia flower essence
>
> White quartz essence or an actual white quartz crystal
>
> Essential oil of eucalyptus
>
> Essential oil of peppermint
>
> A mister filled with spring water

Put 4 drops of gardenia, 3 drops of white quartz (or the crystal), 4 drops of eucalyptus, and 4 drops of peppermint in the mister. Shake. Hold the bottle in both hands and ask Archangel Raphael to fill the liquid with high vibrations that powerfully speed healing. Visualize the bottle filled with very bright white light, and then very bright green light.

Candle Burning for Specific Intentions

Simply lighting a candle can be a magical ritual unto itself. You might like to burn a candle to help with any number of intentions, including but not limited to intentions regarding any of the following:

> Banishing
>
> Career
>
> Creativity
>
> Fame/Reputation
>
> Focus
>
> Health
>
> Intuition/Psychic Abilities
>
> Joy
>
> Manifesting
>
> Prosperity
>
> Romance
>
> Spirituality

Once you've chosen your intention, you're ready to begin preparing for your candle ritual.

1: Clarify

Write down your intention in one sentence, as if it's already happened. For example, you might write "I am wealthy beyond my fondest dreams" or "I am vibrantly healthy in every way."

2: Select a Scent or Scents

Look at the list of oils and choose a scent or scents to help manifest your intention. Write down your selection.

3: Select a Color

Here are some color ideas:

Black: banishing, releasing, dissolving

Deep Blue: intuition, psychic abilities, success, harmony, peace

Green: health, healing, wealth, heart-opening

Lavender: physical beauty, spirituality, harmony

Orange: harmony, warmth, harvest, fruition, sexuality

Red: passion, fame, strength, courage, success, vibrant health, victory, connection with the earth

Robin's-Egg Blue: communication, joy, lightness, self-expression

Violet/Purple: spirituality, inner beauty, magic

White: purity, protection, manifestation, healing

Yellow: energy, clarity, joy, courage, personal power

For more ideas, see the appendix.

4: Obtain Your Candle

Choose or make a soy or other vegetable wax candle.

If you make it, color it and scent it with your chosen color and scent(s). If you purchase it, you can either find a candle with your chosen color and scent, or just a candle with your chosen color. You can then anoint your candle with your chosen scents later (see next step).

As an alternative to getting a colored candle, you can get a white or off-white candle and place it in a colored glass jar or candleholder.

5: Prepare Your Candle

Carve the words of your intention into the candle with a pencil, nail, or something else that works. You can use the entire sentence or you can just choose a word that summarizes your intention, such as "romance," "wealth," "release," or "health." If you're going to anoint your candle with essential oil, put a few (or more, according to your preference) drops of your chosen oil(s) in a carrier oil such as sunflower or olive oil. Then lightly smooth this oil over the entire surface of the candle (except the bottom and the wick) with your fingers. Alternatively, use a paper towel to apply the oil if you're not sure if the essential oils will irritate your skin.

6: Empower Your Candle

Use one of the following two ways: (a) hold it in both hands and visualize and/or feel your intended outcome as if it has already manifested, then mentally direct the energy generated by this visualization into the candle, or (b) use the three secrets empowerment.

7: Light Your Candle

If you're burning the candle to manifest something, burn it during the waxing moon. If you're burning it to release or banish something, burn it during the waning moon. Once you extinguish it, you can just burn it casually whenever you're home and you feel like having some candlelight. Or, if you'd like to speed its magic, burn it whenever you're home until it burns all the way down. Every time you light it, say a quick prayer or do a quick visualization of your intended outcome.

11

Blessings, Protections & Other Rituals

IF YOU'VE READ this far, you've already been familiarized with a number of blessings, protections, and rituals you can do in your home. Well, here are some more! But first, let's explore the topic of ritual a bit more deeply.

Ritual works with nature on the many different levels of the subtle realms, helping to elicit all the beauty, power, and success that already exist in seed form within our hearts. As Marina Medici says in *Good Magic*:

> A good magician, then, is like a good gardener. He knows that changing a rose into another flower is not possible, and that if ever it could be achieved, it would be, at best, just a game. He knows that his job is to sort the weeds from the flowers and to help the flowers grow.

The seeds and the flowers are the true desires of our heart. The weeds are fears, limiting beliefs, and false, externally imposed desires. When we get very clear and focused on our intentions in a positive way, and when our intentions are in alignment with who we really are (the spark of divinity within), our rituals will always succeed.

The activities in this chapter can help you deeply align yourself and your home with all that your heart truly desires and create the space for it to manifest in your life.

Before you perform any of these rituals, you might like to prepare in the following ways. Take as much time as you need with each step, and take the preparatory time to begin to connect with your intuition and the subtler energetic realms.

1. To avoid self-consciousness or energetic interference, make sure you're alone or that the only people present are willing participants in the ritual. (With some of the rituals, you'll need the entire house to yourself, but other simpler ones will just require a room.)

2. Unplug and/or turn off your phone(s).

3. Shower or bathe to purify your energy.

4. Meditate by sitting with a straight spine and taking some deep breaths.

5. Take a moment to connect with the earth by visualizing yourself growing roots and drawing up nourishment from the earth, and take a moment to connect with universal energy by visualizing yourself growing branches and drawing down light and air from the sky.

6. Visualize a very bright sphere of white light surrounding you, and ask that your energy field be powerfully sealed and protected. I like to ask Archangel Michael for help on this part, but you can ask whatever being or beings feel right to you, or just visualize and call upon light.

When you're finished with the ritual, say thank you to the magical powers and/or beings that you've summoned and completely release all attachments to the outcome of your workings with total faith that you have been successful. Because magical workings can raise a lot of energy, you might like to ground yourself afterwards. To do this, lie or sit on the ground (or in a chair if necessary) and visualize a shower of light pouring down over you like water, moving downward into the earth and taking all excess energy in your energy field with it. Finally, eat something to further ground you, like nuts, grains, or root vegetables. You can also drink a beer if you're into that sort of thing, as beer is extremely grounding. You might also want to do something to bring yourself back to the everyday world, such as call a friend, check your email, or make dinner.

Blessings

A blessing is a magical rite that lifts and harmonizes the energy in your home, creating a sacred space for your soul to find sanctuary and your dreams to manifest into form.

. . . .

New House Blessing

Moving into a new (or new to you) house or apartment is a magical time. Your life is in a dynamic transition, and performing this powerful new house blessing can help you make it a positive one, as it infuses your new home with all things bright and beautiful. If you're extremely drawn to this blessing, you can perform it even if you've lived at your current location for some time.

Ideally, you would do this ritual before you've moved in your things. But if this isn't possible for any reason, don't worry about it; it'll still be extremely effective. Before you begin, physically clean the space and perform a thorough space clearing like the one on page 42.

Perform this blessing when the moon is between new and full.

INGREDIENTS:

> A bowl of rose petals from as many red, pink, and
> > yellow roses as you can reasonably acquire
> One small red, pink, and green votive
> > or jar candle for every room
> A plate that will fit three candles for each
> > room (unless the candles are in jars)
> A stick of vanilla or rose incense for each room
> An apple for each room

Place three candles in each room, one of each color. Find the most stable way to set each apple on a flat surface (upside down or right-side up), and stick one stick of incense straight up in each so that the apple will catch the falling ash. Set one apple next to each candle arrangement in each room. Stand in a central location or at the front door. With your hands in prayer pose, say:

> *I now call on sweet spirits of divine light. I now
> call on all the positive energies of this home. Thank
> you for blessing me with this beautiful place to
> live. I now perform this blessing as an offering of
> gratitude. May it be a powerful infusion of harmony,
> prosperity, happiness, and love. Thank you.*

Carry the bowl of rose petals into each room, and perform the following:

Light the candles and incense. Stand in a central location or at the main door to the room with your hands in prayer pose. Close your eyes. Say "Harmony" and visualize bright yellow light filling the room. Say "Prosperity" and visualize bright green light filling the room. Say "Happiness" and visualize bright red light filling the room. Say "Love" and visualize bright pink light filling the room. If the visualizations are too challenging for you at this stage, just say the words and let them resound in your mind. Next, open your hands into Reiki mittens (see page 75) and visualize very bright white or rainbow light flowing down from the sky, into the crown of your head, and out from your hands to swirl around and fill the room. Open your eyes and casually sprinkle a handful of petals in the room, letting them fall on the ground and / or furniture.

When you're finished with each room, stand again at your starting location. Close your eyes, and with your hands in prayer pose, visualize bright white light filling and encompassing the house completely in a huge sphere of light. See this sphere spin in a clockwise direction, and know that this light is sealing the positive energies into your home. When the visualization feels complete, say:

> *It is done. Thank you, thank you,*
> *thank you. Blessed be. And so it is.*

Open your eyes and release your hands. Allow the candles to continue to burn for at least as long as the incense sticks are still burning. If you feel like it and it's safe, you can let the candles continue to burn until they go out naturally, or you can light them again periodically until they burn all the way down. Leave the petals for at least twelve hours but no longer than twenty-four hours. Dispose of them in outside soil, a compost heap, or a yard waste bin so that they can return to the earth. Dispose of the apples in the same way.

. . . .

House Blessing

You might like to perform this blessing every January 1, November 1, or any other time you'd like to harmonize, balance, uplift, and create sacred space by calling positive energy into your home.

Begin by performing a thorough cleaning and clearing. Do this blessing when the moon is between new and full, unless you're doing it at the beginning of another cycle, such as the cycle of the solar, lunar, or pagan year, in which case you don't need to worry about the moon phase.

INGREDIENTS:

> A white, off-white, or light pink votive or jar candle for each room (with dish or candleholder if necessary)
>
> Essential oil of cinnamon
>
> ½ cup sunflower oil
>
> Paper towel or paintbrush
>
> A stick of frankincense incense for each room
>
> An incense burner or apple used as an incense burner (see page 182) for each room
>
> A sprig of rosemary tied with a bright red ribbon for each room

Mix sunflower oil with 9 drops of cinnamon oil, and use a paper towel or paintbrush to anoint each candle with the oil, being careful not to irritate your skin with the cinnamon oil. (Cover all but the wick and the base with a thin layer of oil.) Place one candle in each room, along with one stick of incense.

Stand in a central location or at the front door with your hands in prayer pose. Say:

> *I now call on the sweet spirits of divine light. I now*
> *call on the positive and beneficent energies of this*
> *home. I perform this blessing with great joy and*
> *gratitude. I celebrate and consecrate the sacred space*
> *that is my home. May all good energies swirl within.*
> *May all good energies dwell within. Thank you.*

Carry the rosemary sprigs in a dish or basket with you as you go into each room. While you're in each room, perform the following:

Light the candle and incense. Stand at a central location or at the main door to the room with your hands in prayer pose. Close your eyes and say:

> *May all good energies swirl within.*
> *May all good energies dwell within.*

Open your hands into Reiki mittens (see page 75) and visualize very bright, sparkly, golden-white light coming down from above, through the top of your head, and out through your hands to fill the room. Visualize the light swirling around in a clockwise direction and filling the entire space—even the nooks, crannies, and corners. Open your eyes and place one rosemary sprig in the room, possibly beside the candle and incense.

When you're finished with each room, go back to the beginning location and stand with your hands in prayer pose. Visualize very bright, sparkly, golden-white light filling and surrounding the entire house in a huge sphere. See the sphere begin to spin in a clockwise direction, and know that the positive energies you've summoned are now sealed within the space. Say:

> *I now call on four angels to stand at the compass*
> *points of this sphere of light, to watch over it*
> *and contain all good energies within it.*

Visualize these angels watching over the energy of your home, and mentally thank them. When the visualization feels complete, say:

> *It is done. Thank you, thank you,*
> *thank you. Blessed be. And so it is.*

Open your eyes. Allow the incense to burn all the way down, and allow the candles to burn for at least two hours. If you like, you can also let the candles burn all the way down, or extinguish them and relight them periodically until they burn all the way down. The rosemary sprigs can stay until the next blessing, or you can dispose of them after one week. If you dispose of them, make sure you remove the ribbon and place them either outside in the soil, in a compost heap, or in a yard waste bin so that they can return to the earth.

. . . .

Simple House Blessing

Perhaps you'd like to bless your home but you aren't in the mood to buy a bunch of supplies or perform an extensive ritual. Or maybe you'd like a quick refresher between blessings. Either way, this would be the blessing for you. This would also be a good one to do if you've never performed a ritual before and you'd like to start simple. But don't be fooled: this ritual's simplicity does not diminish its potency.

You can perform this ritual anytime. Before you begin, tidy up, do a quick cleaning, and perform a quick cleansing ritual.

INGREDIENTS:

12 sticks of frankincense or Nag Champa incense

A small dish

A pot or bowl with dirt or potting soil in it

9 sprigs of fresh rosemary

Ribbon or string

Tie the rosemary into a bundle with the string so that it can be hung like an ornament. Stand in a central location or near the front door. Put your hands in prayer pose and say:

> *I call on angels, fairies, and divine beings*
> *of light. You are welcome here.*

Light all the incense sticks and hold them all in a bundle like a smudge stick. Hold the dish under it to catch the burning embers and ash. Move through the house quickly, staying in each room long enough to repeat: "I call on angels, fairies, and divine beings of light. You are welcome here." Return to the central location and put the incense bundle in the potted soil with the burning ends pointing straight up so that any ashes or burning embers will fall into the soil. Place the incense bundle just outside the front door, or, if it's windy or makes you feel more comfortable, place it just inside, at or near the front door. Hold the rosemary bundle in both hands and say:

> *This home is blessed, and all good things*
> *shall flourish within its walls.*

Hang the rosemary bundle on the outside of the front door or above the inside of the front door. Hold your hands in prayer pose, visualize a ring of white light encircling your home, and say:

> *It is done. Thank you, thank you,*
> *thank you. Blessed be. And so it is.*

After the incense bundle has burned all the way down, place the soil and ashes at the base of a tree in your yard or another outdoor setting.

Protections

It's of utmost importance that you and your loved ones feel safe in your home. Protections create an aura of safety from all forms of intrusion and harm, both physical and energetic. (But you should still lock your doors, as it's always best to ask the etheric realm and the physical realm to work together as a team.) A protection also promotes an atmosphere of safety, which soothes stress and anxiety, and therefore enhances harmony and balance on all levels.

. . . .

Aqua Aura Home Protection

This is a highly effective protection that not only keeps out all forms of negativity, it also attunes your space to a whimsical, fairylike vibration in which miracles and magic flourish. The one drawback is that aqua auras can be a bit pricey—not diamond-and-ruby pricey, but pricey as semi-precious gemstones go. If you love this ritual but you don't want to spring for the aqua auras, it will definitely work with white quartz points too, though it will be a bit less whimsical. Or, perhaps you could do half and half.

INGREDIENTS:

8 aqua aura quartz points

A compass

A spade or other digging tool

After cleansing your crystals (see gemstone chapter), hold them in both hands and ask that they be charged with powerfully protective vibes. You might visualize and/or feel this happening in the form of sparkly, swirling energy filling and surrounding them. You'll very likely be able to feel them vibrating with power in your hands during this time.

Now bury each crystal outside around the perimeter of the space you're protecting. Use a compass in order to bury one at the north point of the property, and then continue in a clockwise direction and bury one at the northeast, east, southeast, south, southwest, west, and northwest points respectively. They should all be pointing up and just a tiny bit outward. Then stand at the front door, facing out, and put your hands in Jupiter mudra (see page 73) and extend your arms straight out so that you are pointing straight ahead and your straight arms are parallel with the ground. With your eyes wide open, stare straight ahead and chant the word *protection* sixteen times.

· ·

Garlic and Yarrow Home Protection

This protection works especially well to keep out ill wishes and negative influences. If you feel concerned about bad energy coming from a specific person or group of people, or if you'd like to prevent earthbound entities or any other form of negative etheric or otherworldly energy from entering your home, this would be the protection to perform. This protection can also work well to keep bad dreams away, provided the bad dreams are coming from an external source, such as someone thinking bad thoughts about you or wishing ill upon you.

Do this protection when the moon is full or very close to full, unless it's an emergency, in which case I recommend that you do it right away, regardless of the moon phase. It's best to begin with a thorough cleansing. Also, if you feel you have one or more stubborn earthbound entities living with you, I suggest that you first perform the spirit version of the banishing an unwanted houseguest or resident ritual (see page 203). Then you can do this one to make sure they stay away.

INGREDIENTS:

A red candle

4 cloves of garlic

8 pins with red heads

4 tablespoons dried yarrow in a
ceramic, glass, or metal bowl

1–4 potted plants if necessary (see below)

Assemble the candle, garlic, pins, and yarrow in a central location or at your altar. Light the candle. With your hands in prayer position, say:

> *I call on ten thousand angels and divine*
> *beings of light. Through me, please charge*
> *these ingredients with protective power.*

Move your hands into Reiki mittens (see page 75), with your palms directed toward the pins, yarrow, and garlic. Allow energy to flow through the top of your head, to your heart, and out through your hands to fill the yarrow and garlic with the protective power you have summoned. Now, stick two pins in each clove of garlic. They should move across the narrow side of the clove and form an *X*, with both the points and the heads sticking out both sides.

Now you're going to bury one clove of garlic on each of the four sides of your house. If possible, bury each one in the earth, close to the outside wall of your house. If this isn't possible, place a potted plant outside and bury the clove in the potted plant. If this also isn't possible (if you're in an apartment, for example), place a potted plant inside your house and bury the garlic in it. You might do this in any combination; for example, you might bury the clove in the earth on two sides of your house and inside in a potted plant on two other sides of your house. Each time you bury a clove, put one tablespoon of yarrow on top of it before you cover it up. Once you cover it up, face outward and do the expelling mudra (see page 70) nine times, each time saying "Ong so hung" to align you with the infinite power of the Divine. If you're worried about what the neighbors will think, simply dispense with the expelling mudra and do the mantra mentally.

When you're finished, move back to the candle. Hold your hands in prayer pose and say:

> *Powerful protection is established in this place, and only what is good shall enter and dwell. It is done. Thank you, thank you, thank you. Blessed be. And so it is.*

Blow out the candle.

Simple Angel Protection Ritual

You can do this protection often, and the more you do it, the stronger it becomes. I like to do it every day as a part of my daily meditation.

INGREDIENT:

A white or off-white candle (but even this is unnecessary)

Sit in front of the lit candle with your spine straight. Close your eyes, take some deep breaths, and put your hands in prayer position. Ask Archangel Michael to fill and encompass your home in a sphere of very bright white light. Then ask for him to fine-tune the energy field of your home by sensing any dark areas and powerfully brightening them, burning away and transmuting all negativity. Once this feels complete, ask for a group of angels to encircle your home, directing positive energy inward. See energy flowing from their hands into the center of your home, perpetually raising and preserving the positive vibrations. Then ask for a slightly larger group of angels to encircle that group of angels. See them facing outward, and ask them to powerfully prevent any form of negativity from entering your home. Thank the angels and trust that you and your home are now powerfully protected. Say (mentally or aloud):

> *Thank you, thank you, thank you.*
> *Blessed be. And so it is.*

Other Rituals

These rituals allow you to work with the energy of your home to help manifest a number of different magical intentions.

Perfect Sale Ritual

Perform this for selling a house quickly, perfectly, and for a good price.

As preparation for the ritual, perform the following (it might take a few weeks):

1. Take down all photos of family and friends, and pack them in a box. This will begin the process of removing your energy from the home, and it will also create the space for the new residents.

2. Thoroughly clear out all your clutter. As author Terah Kathryn Collins recommends, ask yourself: "If I moved tomorrow, would I take this with me?" If the answer is no, give it away, throw it away, or sell it ASAP. This will further loosen your energy from the location and create the space for future residents. It will also raise your vibration, which will attract higher-vibrating buyers, as like attracts like.

3. Thoroughly clean. Clean under and behind everything. Even clean the walls. This will further raise the vibration and will help to unstick your energy from the space and prepare it for the new residents.

4. Do a thorough space clearing.

5. Make absolutely positive the front door is sparkling and vibrant. Replace any suffering plants, give it a paint job, replace the address numbers, or do anything else you need to do in order to make the front door shine. Remember, the front door is the first impression and the message you are sending out into the world. Its

condition will dictate the quality of buyer you attract.

6. Do all of this with great love and appreciation for the house and for all that it's provided for you (shelter, comfort, joy, etc.). If you don't have a good relationship with the house or don't feel naturally grateful for it, now is the time to turn that around by recognizing and acknowledging all the blessings this home has offered to you. This will likely open your heart and arouse your emotions, perhaps in a bit of a poignant and nostalgic way. Allow yourself to feel these feelings, even crying a bit sometimes if necessary. Letting these feelings come to the surface to be expressed will allow you to fully release the old and make room for beautiful new conditions to flow into your life.

INGREDIENTS:

1 white or off-white candle

A piece of paper

A metallic gold envelope (painted if necessary)

A pen

A white or clear quartz crystal

Light the candle, sit in front of it, and center yourself. Now, really think about the house. Think about all the good times you've had in it and how grateful you are that it has sheltered and cared for you for all this time. Get emotional about it if possible. After all, you're about to manifest a grand farewell to a dear friend. Once you're in touch with your feelings of gratitude, get ready to write down the qualities you'd like the next owner(s) to have. Because the house has been so good to you, you would definitely not want just anyone to live in it. Perhaps you'll write: "The new owner(s) will be caring, responsible, peaceful, loving, really appreciate the home and take good care of it," etc. Once you've finished with this, write the price you'd like to receive underneath. Write it like this: "I receive $_____ or more." Then, under that, write: "Swift, easy, perfect." Sign and date the document, fold it (always folding toward yourself), and seal it in the envelope. Hold the envelope between your two palms and say:

> *Dear home, you have served me well, and I give*
> *thanks. I now fully release you and let you go. May*
> *you be honored and treasured for as long as you live.*

Place the envelope in a closet, drawer, bookshelf, or cupboard somewhere in your synchronicity and miracles area, put the crystal on top of it, and surrender the situation with total confidence and trust. Once the house has sold, thank the universe for your good fortune and place the envelope in the recycling bin.

. . . .

Attracting Love

Before you decide it's time to attract that special someone into your life, it's time for an assessment. Do you love yourself? Do you treat yourself with deep compassion and respect? Of course everyone suffers from occasional challenges in these areas, but if you feel the answer is most often no to either of these questions, you'll only attract someone who doesn't love you and who doesn't treat you with deep compassion and respect. Not only that, but you won't be able to fully offer these things to someone else either. In this case, start by carefully reading *You Can Heal Your Life* by Louise Hay, and come back to this ritual later. I mean it. More than once, if necessary. You might also want to take a course in self-love, start doing yoga or meditating, work with an energy healer, read a different book, or all of the above. What I'm getting at is, there is a prerequisite to this ritual, and it is to cultivate a deep and abiding self-love, whatever you must do and however long it may take. (And it's okay if it takes time. It usually does!)

However, if you do feel ready, this ought to do the trick.

INGREDIENTS:

  2 cups of dried red or pink rose petals or blossoms,
     ground to a fine powder in a coffee grinder,
     food processor, or mortar and pestle

  ¼ cup orris root powder

  1 vial of fancy pink glitter from a craft store

  A red, pink, or white ceramic bowl

  1 pink candle

Ideally, perform this ritual on the first Friday after a new moon, but any Monday, Friday, or Sunday when the moon is between new and full will do. After dark, assemble the ingredients, light the candle, and center yourself. Hold your hands in Reiki mittens (see page 75), palms facing the roses, orris, and glitter, and, as you visualize golden-pink sparkly light coming down through your head, to your heart, and out through your hands into the ingredients, say:

> *I now charge these ingredients with*
> *the bright magnetic light of love.*

Then mix these ingredients together in the bowl. Set the bowl in front of you, and hold the heart-calming mudra (see page 71) as you repeat "Aham prema" nine times. Then go outside and sprinkle the mixture all along the pathway leading to your front door, under your doormat, and outside your front door. Sprinkle any remaining powder elsewhere (outside) around the perimeter of your home. Go back to the candle, hold your hands in prayer pose, and say:

> *It is done. My romantic partner is perfect for me in every way, and he/she is on his/her way to me now. Thank you, thank you, thank you. Blessed be. And so it is.*

. . . .

Attracting Money

INGREDIENTS:

   9 oranges

   A non-plastic bowl big enough for nine oranges

   Gold ribbon

   Green ribbon

   A green candle

   Optional but recommended: a few drops of
      essential oil of cinnamon and/or clove mixed
      with a tablespoon of sunflower oil

Ideally, you would do this ritual on the new moon, but any Thursday or Sunday when the moon is close to new and between new and full will work too.

Assemble all ingredients and center yourself. Carve a dollar sign into the candle. If you're using oil, anoint the candle with it by spreading a thin layer over the entire surface area, excluding the base and wick. Light the candle. Hold your hands in prayer pose, close your eyes, and say:

I call on the angels of abundance.

Direct your open palms toward the oranges and ribbons, and say:

*I charge these ingredients with the magnetic
light of financial prosperity.*

Visualize sparkly green/gold/rainbow light coming down through the top of your head, to your heart, and out your hands into the oranges and ribbons. Now, tie a bow around an orange with one piece of green ribbon and one piece of gold ribbon. Once you've tied it, hold the orange in both hands and say:

*I open the floodgates of abundance and
welcome infinite wealth into my life now.*

Place the orange in the bowl and repeat with each orange. (If any of the bows fall off, don't worry about it—the ritual will work just as well.) When you're finished, hold your hands in prayer pose and say:

*It is done. Thank you, thank you,
thank you. Blessed be. And so it is.*

Place the bowl on your stove, and place the candle next to it. Let the candle burn all the way down or extinguish it and burn it again (as convenient) until it burns all the way down. It's okay to move the oranges and candle when you use your stove, just move them back afterwards. At the full moon or the day after, dispose of the oranges by burying them or placing them in a compost heap or yard waste bin so that they can return to the earth. Or, in this case, it's okay to eat them—just make sure you dispose of the peels in the above-mentioned way. (If you do eat them, you'll be internalizing the magic, which will likely be verrrry interesting in a probably pleasant yet unpredictable way.) Tie the ribbons together into a charm, and hang or place it in your gratitude and prosperity area or hang it on the outside of your front door, the inside doorknob of your front door, or on the wall above the inside of your front door.

. . . .

Attracting an Ideal Career and/or Discovering Your Life Path

This draws upon an old-school feng shui ritual. I personally have experienced great success with it. Years ago, it helped me to discover my path as a magical housekeeper and metaphysical writer.

To prepare, write out all the ideal qualities of your most perfect career ever. You don't have to know what the career is yet, just the qualities. So, for example, you might write: "I work from home, I make $_____ a week or more, I work less than ____ hours per week, I express my unique talents and abilities, I adore the people I work with/for, I am very appreciated, I get to wear whatever I want, etc., etc." If you find yourself thinking, "This is impossible, there's no career that fits this description" or "This is too good to be true," override these thoughts and remind yourself that your desires aren't arbitrary—rather, they are road markers to your perfect success. Allow yourself to honestly and authentically claim your ideal circumstances. Take your time and fine-tune this list according to your inner guidance. What I mean is, be careful that you don't list things just because you think you should want them or fail to list things just because you think you shouldn't want them.

INGREDIENTS:

> A white or off-white candle
>
> A pen
>
> The list of qualities you wrote (as described above)
>
> A blank postcard depicting the ocean, a picture of the ocean that's blank on the back, or a picture of yourself in front of the ocean that's blank on the back
>
> A white quartz crystal point
>
> A bright or deep red 100 percent natural fiber cloth, the exact size of the top of your mattress or a tiny bit smaller (perhaps a table cloth or sheet)

Take the mattress off your bed so that the box spring is exposed. Then assemble the ingredients, light the candle, and center yourself.

With your eyes closed and your hands in prayer pose (see page 69), say:

I summon my ideal career and life path now.

Open your eyes and copy the qualities of your ideal career onto the back of the ocean picture. Go to the career and life path area of your home and place the ocean picture somewhere with the ocean side visible (if you prefer, you can also put it in a drawer or somewhere else where you can't see it, just put it ocean-side up). Place the quartz point near it or above it.

Now, take the red cloth and spread it over the top of your box spring. Stand above it and feel that you've already discovered your ideal career path. As fully as you can, experience the joy this brings. You might also see images in your mind's eye of yourself joyfully at work. Then do the expelling mudra (see page 70) nine times, flicking your fingers toward the cloth as you say the six true words each time ("Om ma ni pad me hum").

Finish with your hands in prayer pose and your eyes closed, and say:

> *Thank you, thank you, thank you.*
> *Blessed be. And so it is.*

Put the mattress back on your bed so that the cloth is sandwiched between the mattress and box spring; the magic will infuse your aura as you sleep. Extinguish the candle.

. . . .

Happy Home Ritual

This is the ritual to do when you'd like to create more harmony and happiness in your home, and overcome old, stagnant energy, uncomfortably challenging relationships, and/or chronic discord of any kind. This is also a good one to do to help heal your romantic relationship with a live-in partner if it feels less than harmonious. In some cases, the results might seem a bit more chaotic at first, but know that it's all for the sake of true, lasting harmony. In other words, this is not a Band-Aid cure: buried issues will come to the surface so that they can be sorted out and dealt with in the best possible way.

First, thoroughly clean the house and clear the energy. Then you're ready to begin. Do this when the moon is in Cancer or Libra (check a magical or astrological almanac or look online), on any day other than Tuesday, when the moon is between new and full.

INGREDIENTS:

Approximately ½ cup dried nettles

Approximately ½ cup dried elecampane

One orange or peach-colored votive candle for every room

A small plate or platelike candleholder for each room

Essential oil of tangerine

Essential oil of neroli

2 tablespoons light olive oil

Assemble all ingredients at an altar or central location. Hold your hands in prayer pose and say:

> *I now call on Hestia, the goddess of the hearth. I*
> *now request your powerful help with this ritual to*
> *create harmony and happiness within these walls.*

Now hold your hands over the ingredients and feel a deep wellspring of harmony and joy flowing in from the top of your head, down to your heart, and out through your hands into the ingredients. You might visualize the ingredients being filled with light. Carve this symbol, the rune Ger (or Jera), into each candle:

It represents natural balance and the cycles of nature, and it also helps reveal and heal any buried issues and blocks to true harmony. Then, in a small container, put 9 drops of each essential oil in 2 tablespoons of olive oil and blend. Anoint each candle with the oil by spreading a thin layer of oil over the entire surface, excluding the base and wick. Place each candle on a small plate and sprinkle a small amount of nettles and ele-campane around each base. One by one, place a candle in each room and light it. After you light each candle, hold your hands in prayer pose, and with your eyes closed, say:

Happy, sweet, harmonious, blessed.

When you're finished lighting all the candles, go back to the central location and say:

Thank you, thank you, thank you.
Blessed be. And so it is.

Allow the candles to burn for at least two hours, or let them burn all the way down.

. . . .

Banishing an Unwanted Houseguest or Resident (Human)

Be careful with this one! When performing rituals, it's important to send out only good energy, as all energy you send out comes back to you at least threefold. Believe me, many years ago, when I was young and rebellious, I learned this one the hard way, and it was *no fun*. And so, take great care if this is a person with whom you have issues. (Which I'm guessing it is—I know, psychic, right?)

This ritual is only to be performed if you've tried every other civilized option (asking nicely, asking firmly, etc.) and it hasn't worked. Also, if there's a conflict, check in with yourself to make sure that you're the one with the ethical upper hand. Don't go kicking someone out of his or her rightful home, or you'll most definitely be very, very (and I mean *very*) sorry, since that old threefold law, in such a circumstance, is never less than a major bite in the ass.

INGREDIENTS:

> A photocopy of a picture of the person you wish to banish
>
> 1 tablespoon black pepper
>
> 1 tablespoon garlic powder
>
> Something in which to burn the picture,
>   like an old pot or bowl
>
> A candle

Perform this ritual the day after the full moon.

Light the candle and center yourself. Close your eyes. Call upon the most pure and spiritual aspect of your being, the part of you that knows no conflict and knows only love. From this part of you, call upon the higher self of the person you wish to banish. See if you can overlook your differences and really feel warmth and good wishes toward this person. Once you've done this, visualize yourself shaking hands with this person and saying, "I thank you for all that you have taught me. Now it's time for us to part ways." Then wish this person only good as you visualize him/her turning around and walking away until out of sight. As you do this, imagine that he/she is walking toward a bright and beautiful future, and continually wish him/her well in his/her new life and residence.

Open your eyes and immediately light the picture on fire. As it burns, visualize this person's energy being utterly purified and removed from your home. When only ash remains, mix the ash with the pepper and garlic powder. Go outside and sprinkle the mixture around the outside of your house or property (whichever feels right). If this isn't possible because you have common walls with other homes, sprinkle the mixture in a line across the outside of all the doorways and windowpanes that lead to the outside. The amount you sprinkle should be just skimpy enough so that it's not easily noticeable. If any mixture is remaining, flush it down the toilet. Go back to the still-burning candle and say:

> *It is done. Thank you, thank you,*
> *thank you. Blessed be. And so it is.*

Extinguish the candle, clean up any leftover evidence of the ritual, and wash your hands. The person should be gone within two weeks.

· ·

Banishing an Unwanted Houseguest or Resident (Spirit)

There are two kinds of what we might call "ghosts," and they are very different from each other. There's the spirit guide variety—the type that can be described as bright, beneficent, and helpful—and then there's the earthbound entity variety, the type that gets stuck between realms because of confusion, addiction, guilt, unfinished business, or some other sort of unhealthy attachment to the physical realm. You're very likely dealing with the latter if you experience any of the following in your home:

- A depressing, sad, and/or heavy feeling

- Areas that stay mysteriously cold

- A feeling that the lights are perpetually dimmed

- A feeling of being profoundly drained or unfocused

- Clunking, scratching, nighttime footsteps, or any other strange noises

- A sudden, unexplained addiction that just doesn't seem like you (e.g., you suddenly want

to buy cigarettes and you've never been a
smoker)

• The rearranging or mysterious disappearance
of objects

• Things that turn on or off by themselves

• A suspicion that a deceased former resident is
hanging around

If these are occurring, do a thorough space clearing and
then perform this banishing ritual ASAP, which will help the
ghost move along to the next realm.

INGREDIENTS:

A white candle for each room

A few drops of essential oil of angelica (or actual
dried angelica) mixed with sunflower oil

Copal incense

An incense holder (or something that
works as one) for each room

Important note: if you live with any animals, put them outside or find somewhere else for them to stay during this ritual.

When the moon is between full and new, after dark, assemble all the ingredients in a central location. Anoint each candle
with the sunflower/angelica oil by spreading a thin layer over
the entire surface area, excluding the base and wick, and place
one candle in each room, with one stick of incense. Alternatively, you can sprinkle the dried angelica in a circle around
each candle on a plate or candleholder. Light the candle and
one stick of the incense in the first room, hold your hands in
prayer pose (see page 69), and say:

> *Archangel Michael, I call on you. Please*
> *remove any and all earthbound spirits from*
> *this space and take them to the light.*

Repeat this process in each room, being very aware of fire safety. When you're finished, take a good look and make sure everything is burning *very* safely, and then go outside of the house for one to two hours. When you return, turn on all the lights, extinguish and dispose of the candles, open all the doors and windows, and turn on all the faucets and showers for one minute. Then put everything back to normal and play very dynamic and uplifting music loudly to move the energy around even more. (Yes, disco is okay.) Thank Archangel Michael for his help. Then invite a bunch of angels and/or all the good spirits and beings you can think of to protect the space and keep it free of lower energies.

Conclusion

Go Forth, Magical Housekeeper!

CONSIDER YOURSELF INITIATED into the holy order of magical housekeepers! You now realize that your home is an alchemical tool of manifestation, and you recognize it as your palace, your oasis, and the place where you nurture yourself and reverently honor your true divine essence.

To strengthen and solidify your fresh perspective and newly discovered powers, it will help to continually remind yourself of the main principles behind magical housekeeping: that everything is connected, and that there's no separation between the physical and the ethereal. In other words, your external landscape mirrors your internal landscape and vice versa. It's simple, really: What do you want to experience? Harmony? Romance? Luxury? Begin by clearly setting your intentions. Then create these qualities in your home environment (and perhaps reinforce your efforts with a ritual or two), and your life experience will naturally follow suit.

But manifesting the conditions we want in our lives is only part of the story. What we're really doing when we keep house in a magical way is living consciously and compassionately. We're making choices that are not just for our highest good, they are also for the highest good of all—plants, animals, our loved ones, and the entire planet. Knowing that we're part of everything and honoring this knowledge through our choices and actions breathes beauty and meaning into our lives. And it's cyclical and symbiotic: living consciously and compassionately is the real key to true success and lasting joy.

All of existence is a unified sea of energy. When you think of your home as part of this sea, you can see how magical housekeeping can shift the tide—not just for you, but also, eventually, for everyone and everything. The ripples of peace that emanate from your little corner of the globe can gain momentum and turn into very powerful waves. So go forth, magical housekeeper! Save the planet and establish world peace, starting with your own heart and your own home!

Appendix

Color Correspondences

Beige or Tan: grounding, comforting, light, thoughtful, sensible

Black: magical power, banishment, fluidity, the water element

Blue, Bright: health enhancing, connection with the healing aspects of the unconscious mind, self-expression

Blue, Light: cooling, dreamy, enhances gentleness and gentle self-expression, cools passions

Brown, Dark or Chocolate: the earth element with a little of the water element; deep, nourishing stability with a touch of fluidity

Brown: the earth element, grounding, stabilizing

Cream: like the qualities of white but a bit warmer and more receptive

Gold, Metallic: prosperity enhancing, enlists the help of the Divine, aligned with sun energy

Green, Bright or Kelly: vibrant health, wealth, love

Green, Forest: deep, health enhancing, wealth drawing, stabilizing, nurturing

Green, Honeydew: grounding, uplifting, energizing, health enhancing

Green, Sage: promotes rationality, centeredness, and calm; does not enhance passion (keep this in mind for the bedroom and love/marriage area)

Grey: emotion mixed with rationality, contained fluidity

Indigo: connection with intuition, the unconscious, and divine guidance

Lavender: dreamy, magical, soothing, inspirational; associated with physical beauty and the spiritual aspects of romance

Orange: relaxed power, confidence, the elements of earth and fire

Peach: the receptive, sweet, nurturing, and warm aspects of romantic love; also enhances self-love and self-acceptance; promotes peace

Pink, Bright or Fuschia: sexual attractiveness and seduction; good for beginning stages of entering the dating world and for enhancing your self-image

Pink, Bubblegum: very sweet, heart-opening, and romance enhancing; melting the heart

Pink, Pale or Baby: sweet, gentle, youthful aspects of romantic love; femininity; the beginning stages of warming the heart

Red, Bright: the fire element, energy, passion, courage, health

Red, Deep or Brick: good for grounding and confidence

Silver, Metallic: enlists the help of the Divine, encourages flights of imagination, aligned with moon energy

Teal or Turquoise: vibrant health, the immune system, self-expression, heart-opening, upward movement, wealth

Travertine: precision, authority, calm, discernment, the masculine manifestations of the Divine

Violet or Purple: otherworldly beauty, magical realms, wealth and abundance, connection with the Divine

White: ideas, precision, mental powers, purity, cleanliness, lightness, simplicity, help from the angels

Yellow, Bright or Goldenrod: energizing and stabilizing

Yellow, Light or Butter Cream: bright, cheery, grounding, inspirational, sweet, receptive, soothing

Bibliography

Ashley-Farrand, Thomas. *Mantra Meditation*. Boulder, CO: Sounds True, 2004.

Barnard, Tanya, and Sarah Kramer. *The Garden of Vegan*. Vancouver: Arsenal Pulp Press, 2002.

Campbell, Jeff. *Speed Cleaning*. New York: Dell, 1991.

Chevallier, Andrew. *Encyclopedia of Herbal Medicine*. New York: Dorling Kindersley, 2000.

Cobb, Linda. *Talking Dirty with the Queen of Clean*, 2nd ed. New York: Pocket Books, 1998.

Collins, Terah Kathryn. *The Western Guide to Feng Shui*. Carlsbad, CA: Hay House, 1996.

———. *The Western Guide to Feng Shui for Romance*. Carlsbad, CA: Hay House, 2004.

———. *The Western Guide to Feng Shui: Room by Room*. Carlsbad, CA: Hay House, 1999.

Cousens, Gabriel. *Conscious Eating*. Berkeley, CA: North Atlantic Books, 2000.

Cunningham, Scott. *Cunningham's Encyclopedia of Magical Herbs*. St. Paul, MN: Llewellyn, 1985.

———. *Magical Aromatherapy: The Power of Scent*. St. Paul, MN: Llewellyn, 1989.

Cunningham, Scott, and David Harrington. *The Magical Household*. St. Paul, MN: Llewellyn, 1983.

Bibliography

De Luca, Diana. *Botanica Erotica: Arousing Body, Mind, and Spirit.* Rochester, VT: Healing Arts Press, 1998.

Dugan, Ellen. *Cottage Witchery.* Woodbury, MN: Llewellyn, 2005.

Geddess, Neil, and Alicen Geddess-Ward. *Faeriecraft.* Carlsbad, CA: Hay House, 2005.

Ginsberg, Allen. *Howl and Other Poems.* San Francisco: City Lights, 1956.

Hay, Louise. *You Can Heal Your Life.* Carlsbad, CA: Hay House, 1984.

Illes, Judika. *The Element Encyclopedia of 5000 Spells.* London: HarperElement, 2004.

Katie, Byron, and Michael Katz. *I Need Your Love—Is That True?* New York: Three Rivers Press, 2006.

———. *Loving What Is: Four Questions That Can Change Your Life.* New York: Three Rivers Press, 2003.

Kennedy, David Daniel. *Feng Shui for Dummies.* Hoboken, NJ: Wiley Publishing, 2001.

Kingston, Karen. *Clear Your Clutter with Feng Shui.* New York: Broadway Books, 1998.

———. *Creating Sacred Space with Feng Shui.* New York: Broadway Books, 1997.

Kloss, Jethro. *Back to Eden.* Loma Linda: Back to Eden, 1939.

Linn, Denise. *Feng Shui for the Soul.* Carlsbad, CA: Hay House, 2000.

———. *Space Clearing A–Z.* Carlsbad, CA: Hay House, 2001.

Lust, John. *The Herb Book.* New York: Bantam, 1979.

Medici, Marina. *Good Magic.* New York: Fireside, 1988.

Melody. *Love Is in the Earth*. Wheat Ridge, CO: Earth-Love Publishing House, 1995.

Rattana, Guru. *Transitions to a Heart-Centered World*. Sunbury, PA: Yoga Technology, 1988.

Scheffer, Mechthild. *The Encyclopedia of Bach Flower Therapy*. Rochester, VT: Healing Arts Press, 2001.

Spitzer, K. D. "Magic Squares." *Llewellyn's 2009 Magical Almanac*. Woodbury, MN: Llewellyn, 2008.

Sunset Publishing Corporation. *The Sunset Western Garden Book*. Menlo Park, CA: Sunset Publishing Corporation, 2001.

Van Praagh, James. *Ghosts Among Us: Uncovering the Truth About the Other Side*. New York: HarperOne, 2008.

Virtue, Doreen. *Archangels and Ascended Masters*. Carlsbad, CA: Hay House, 2003.

———. *Fairies 101*. Carlsbad, CA: Hay House, 2007.

———. *Healing with the Fairies*. Carlsbad, CA: Hay House, 2001.

———. *The Lightworker's Way*. Carlsbad, CA: Hay House, 1997.

Virtue, Doreen, and Becky Prelitz. *Eating in the Light*. Carlsbad, CA: Hay House, 2001.

Wolfe, Amber. *Personal Alchemy*. St. Paul, MN: Llewellyn, 1993.

Wolverton, B. C. *How to Grow Fresh Air: 50 Houseplants that Purify Your Home or Office*. New York: Penguin Books, 1996.

Index

Index

Index

Index

Index

To Write to the Author

If you wish to contact the author or would like more information about this book, please write to the author in care of Llewellyn Worldwide Ltd. and we will forward your request. Both the author and the publisher appreciate hearing from you and learning of your enjoyment of this book and how it has helped you. Llewellyn Worldwide Ltd. cannot guarantee that every letter written to the author can be answered, but all will be forwarded. Please write to:

Tess Whitehurst
c/o Llewellyn Worldwide Ltd.
2143 Wooddale Drive
Woodbury, MN 55125-2989

Please enclose a self-addressed stamped envelope for reply,
or $1.00 to cover costs. If outside the U.S.A., enclose an
international postal reply coupon.

Many of Llewellyn's authors have websites with additional information and resources. For more information, please visit our website:

http://www.llewellyn.com